THE GULF STOCK EXCHANGE CRASH
The Rise and Fall of the Souq Al-Manakh

THE GULF STOCK EXCHANGE CRASH
THE RISE AND FALL OF THE SOUQ AL-MANAKH

FIDA DARWICHE

CROOM HELM
London • Sydney • Dover, New Hampshire

Croom Helm Ltd, Provident House, Burrell Row,
Beckenham, Kent BR3 1AT

Croom Helm Australia Pty Ltd, Suite 4, 6th Floor,
64–76 Kippax Street, Surry Hills, NSW 2010 Australia

British Library Cataloguing in Publication Data

Darwiche, Fida
The Gulf stock exchange crash: the rise
and fall of the Souq Al-Manakh.
1. Souq Al-Manakh
I. Title
332.64 2536 HG5712.S6/

ISBN 0-7099-4534-5

Croom Helm, 51 Washington Street, Dover, New Hampshire, 03820 USA

Library of Congress Cataloging-in-Publication Data

Darwiche, Fadwa Adel.
The Gulf stock exchange.

Bibliography: p.
Includes index.
1. Gulf stock exchange (Kuwait, Kuwait)—history.
2. Stock-exchange—Kuwait—history. 3. Stock-exchange—
Arabia—history. I. Title.
HG719.G85D37 1986 332.64′25367 86-6406
ISBN 0-7099-4534-5

Filmset by Mayhew Typesetting, Bristol, England
Printed and bound in Great Britain by Mackays of Chatham Ltd, Kent

Contents

List of Figures and Tables

Foreword

Introduction

1. Kuwaiti Public Companies 1950–80 1

2. Gulf Public Companies 1976–82 20

3. Gulf Stock Exchange 54

4. Gulf Stock Exchange Crisis 86

Bibliography 145

Postscript 154

Index 157

Figures and Tables

Figures

1.1	Structure of the Securities Commission	11
1.2	Structure of the Securities Administration	12
1.3	Movement of Share Prices, 1976–82	16

Tables

1.1	Kuwaiti Public Companies, 1952–80	6
1.2	Maximum and Minimum Share Prices, 1976–82	17
2.1	Gulf Public Companies, 1976–82	28
2.2	Differentials Between Face and Market Values of Shares	35
2.3	Gulf Company Profit and Loss Figures, 1979–83	47
3.1	Differential Between Face and Market Value of Shares of Gulf Companies in January 1984 on Al-Manakh	64
3.2	Bahraini Public Companies, 1957–81	73

Foreword

The Kuwait stock market attracted considerable attention in the financial press even before the crash of Souq Al-Manakh, the unofficial exchange. Kuwait became, during the 1970s and early 1980s, by far the most important centre in the Arab World for stock market transactions, and the only state in the Gulf with a diversified financial services sector. The market provided finance not only for Kuwaiti ventures, but also for companies from other Gulf states, where equity capital could not be easily raised. Shares in these so called Gulf companies were traded in a parallel market, the unregulated Souq Al-Manakh.

It is this parallel market, rather than the official Kuwait stock exchange, which is the subject of this book. Fida Darwiche's study is the first detailed examination of the factors which resulted in the growth of the Souq Al-Manakh and its subsequent collapse. Hitherto all of the accounts of the market have been in the form of short articles, mostly written by financial journalists, rather than more thorough investigations. Fida Darwiche has produced a serious academic study of the market, and its significance for Kuwait. It seems destined to be the definitive work on the subject.

The book should be of interest to all those concerned with economic development and political change on the Arabian Peninsula, especially area studies specialists from outside, and government officials, bankers and academics from within the region. The work is of wider interest, however, as it provides a fascinating case study of the hazards of operating in a completely free and unregulated market. As such it should be of interest to financial analysts generally, and not just those involved in the Arab World or the Middle East.

Although this book is based on a manuscript originally submitted as an M.Phil. for the University of Exeter, which I had the privilege to externally examine, it is no staid academic treatise. The Souq Al-Manakh had a colourful, if chequered history, and the wheeler-dealers who participated in the market were often flamboyant characters. Fida Darwiche interviewed many of the major participants in the market herself, and manages to convey some of the excitement of the deals struck. The dealers and investors were often natural financial innovators, and it is interesting to observe the emergence of new financial instruments which helped market transactions gain momentum, with gains for all. Unfortunately one of the main instruments, the post-dated cheque, was to be the undoing of the market once prices started to level, and heady conditions gave way to a loss of confidence.

Fida Darwiche's study is an excellent example of what a well researched financial history should be. The author demonstrates that she is fully conversant wth her subject, and has a good grasp of financial technicalities. Yet the book is written in a style which should be accessible to a wide readership, and not just those from an economic or financial background. The work represents a superb attempt to chronicle one facet of contemporary Arab economic history. It is to be hoped other similar studies will appear in due course. Certainly it is encouraging to note that Fida Darwiche is continuing her studies at the University of Exeter into Arab Gulf finance to doctoral level.

Rodney Wilson
Senior Lecturer in the Economics of the Middle East
and Pro-Director of the Middle East Centre,
University of Durham.

To my dear Father and Mother
without whose patience,
encouragement and understanding
this work would not have come to light

Introduction

Four years after the collapse of the Gulf stock exchange in Kuwait, better known as the Souq Al-Manakh, and two years after the closure of the stock exchange itself, the crisis has remained at the centre of economic and political controversy in Kuwait and the other Gulf states as well as in Arab and foreign finance institutions, and it is likely to remain so for many years to come.

I believe there is virtually no Arab reader interested in public affairs or Western reader keen on international economic current affairs for whom the name 'Souq Al-Manakh' will not ring a bell in their mind. However, except for the fact that the catastrophe cost US$92 billion when it occurred in 1982, I doubt whether many people realise the wider-dimension of economic and political elements involved in the crisis.

Had the Gulf stock exchange crisis been a short-lived affair and limited to the stock exchange itself, I would certainly not have taken it up as the subject-matter for a book. My choice of it was based on the fact that the crisis is an embodiment of the major elements and developments which reflect, both economically and politically, the era of the oil boom in the Arab Gulf region and represent, in a certain manner, the negative aspects related to the squandering of the oil wealth.

He who cares to follow the story of the Gulf stock exchange in Kuwait from its beginning in 1976 up to the crash in September 1982 with its economic and political implications, will discover that the theme of the story parallels the ups and downs of the era of the oil boom and subsequent bust.

International oil prices began to escalate in the autumn of 1973 and by 1976, rates of monetary flow to the oil-producing Arab Gulf states were doubling, trebling and quadrupling in an unprecedented manner. In 1976, the first Gulf joint-stock companies were established through the initiative of Kuwaiti investors. Such companies were soon to dominate the economic scene in the UAE and Bahrain, and to impose their presence — though illegitimately — in Kuwait.

In 1980 international oil prices peaked at the level of US$34 for a barrel of crude compared to barely US$2 only seven years earlier. By this date the predominance of the Gulf joint-stock companies had necessitated the creation of the Gulf stock-exchange in Kuwait under the name 'Souq Al-Manakh', and lesser stock markets in the United Arab Emirates and Bahrain. This period witnessed a large-scale boom in share trading throughout the Gulf.

As we shall see, the immediate post-1980 period witnessed the 'golden era' of the Gulf stock exchange which extended throughout 1981 and into the first months of 1982.

This was followed by a countercurrent, as 1982 signalled the beginning of an economic recession in the Gulf, directly attributable to the lower oil prices which had been introduced in 1981. Likewise this was the beginning of the end of the Souq Al-Manakh so that by September 1982 the crash occurred.

At the political level the Iraq-Iran war looms large. The hostilities began in September 1980, and by the time the recession reared its ugly head in 1982, a general conviction that no end to the war was in sight prevailed throughout the Gulf. Thus the recession, combined with the fear that the zone of fighting might widen, began to create a deep feeling of non-confidence and non-security in the circles of finance and commerce and in fact permeated all market dealings. This was reflected in the Gulf stock exchange in the form of feverish speculation, fuelled by the drive for quick profit-making which hastened the collapse of the stock market.

The collapse also helped to unmask the drawbacks of well entrenched economic practices hitherto considered legitimate and valid. Foremost among these is the concept of Market Economy and the extent to which the application of this concept within the national economy could be considered safe. It has been demonstrated that had it not been for the government's refusal to intervene forcefully at an early stage, by deciding on the legality of the Gulf stock exchange in Kuwait and by imposing its power on the market and controlling its activity, the catastrophe would probably not have occurred at all. But for the sake of upholding economic freedom the government found it difficult to intervene strongly.

Application of this principle to the letter has brought the dangers which can arise from the lack of centralised economic planning to the fore. In the absence of programmed economic investment under state control in productive fields such as agriculture and industry, surplus money in the hands of individuals was bound to find its way into the wasteful channels of stock exchange gambling. In this manner vast individual savings were squandered.

The crisis and its aftermath also unveiled the dangerous dependence of the private sector upon government spending and the more precarious dependence of the state on a single source of income — revenues from oil exports. With the deterioration of international oil prices to US$12 for a barrel of crude during the first quarter of 1986 from a peak of US$34 in 1980, the governments of the Gulf states have been compelled to adopt successive austerity measures to cut down public spending — a matter which certainly jeopardises the position of the private sector. In Kuwait particularly, the government finds itself in a dilemma between its desire to increase public spending in order to bail out companies brought to the edge of bankruptcy by the stock exchange crisis, and the necessity of slashing public spending as revenues from oil dwindle. This has led to a political struggle between those who favour the use of state funds to compensate those who suffered financially as a result of the stock market collapse, and those who believe that surplus state funds should be preserved as a cushion against leaner times as oil prices continue to fall.

Thus the aftermath of the Gulf stock exchange crash continues to fuel controversy on economics and politics and the outlook for the future.

This was the reason for my choice of the subject, and in the pages of this book the reader will find that I have dealt with the historical background of stock trading in Kuwait, the United Arab Emirates and Bahrain; the developments leading to the establishment of the Gulf stock exchange; the activity of the stock exchange and its financial and legal aspects. I have then examined the collapse of the stock exchange, dissecting the direct and indirect causes, effects, and implications of the catastrophe and ways of repairing the damage. I have striven to present the first documented and comprehensive study of the Gulf stock exchange catastrophe. The reader might wish to know that the prime difficulty I encountered was the lack of reference works on the subject; accordingly I had to depend on sources of a field-study nature.

As the collapse of the Gulf stock exchange will most probably enter the annals of Gulf economic history as an independent chapter, I hope that this book will constitute one of the major reference sources for future students and that the reader will, in the meantime, find it a useful and valuable addition to his or her knowledge.

1

Kuwaiti Public Companies 1950-80

Historical Development

The emergence of the public company heralds a significant transition in the development of modern societies. Private enterprise founded on a small capital base has been eclipsed by the public company with multiple resources. Whereas management enterprise in a private company is limited by the talent and will of the owner, no public company owned by a multitude of shareholders can be run by all shareholders simultaneously.

As a result, the appointment of a separate managerial body became imperative, which released the potential to develop business management skills.[1] With the growth and expansion of the economic structure and the start of economic and social development plans, the road was clear for investors to put their funds into such companies.

Public companies began to spring up in the Gulf, and particularly in Kuwait, after the discovery of oil in the area. Although Kuwaitis, encouraged by the new wealth, began to think along the lines of establishing public companies as early as the fifties, reform of the banking system came first in view of its importance and the high risk involved. The only bank operating throughout Kuwait at the time was the British Bank for the Middle East. Opened in 1941[2] and owned by foreign shareholders, it had a monopoly of all banking business and transactions.

In 1951, a study was undertaken to establish a Kuwaiti national bank that would be owned and run exclusively by nationals. The bank opened on 25th September 1952 with a capital of KD 19,465,875,[3] Kuwait's first public company. As shares were open for public subscription, this heralded the beginning of the country's money market. Encouraged by the success of the venture, investors began to form other public companies. The second was the National Kuwaiti Cinema Company, formed on 5th October 1954 with capital of KD 1,630,263, followed by Kuwaiti Oil Tankers on 19th September 1957, with capital of KD 25,936,605, in which the Kuwaiti government took a 53 per cent stake.[4]

The existence of these three public companies allowed the first buying and selling of shares. Trading in new-company shares became so popular that several newly-formed companies were over-subscribed ten times, a phenomenon which reflected people's strong interest in channelling their savings into good investments. However, the investors' lack of business acumen, combining with the fact that speculation was unknown in this field, meant that the circulation of stocks was limited to what was virtually a closed circle. Not for long. Speculation and deals began to steer a chaotic course, as speculators exploited soaring share prices in order to make quick profits.[5]

In view of this and the zeal of investors to launch further companies, the Kuwaiti government intervened to regulate the incorporation of new companies and dealings in their stock by the first Commercial Companies Act, No. 15/1960.[6] The Act covered joint stock companies, partnerships and joint ventures, as well as companies with assets (limited liability companies and public companies).

The Act stipulated the following with respect to public companies:

1. All public companies formed in the country must be Kuwaiti. The shareholders must be Kuwaiti nationals and the head office located in that country. Notwithstanding this provision, exceptions were allowed with respect to companies outside the banking and insurance sectors. This was so as to allow public companies to respond to contingencies such as the injection of foreign capital and expertise. The Act stipulated that Kuwaiti control should never fall below 51 per cent and that prior authorisation should be had from the government department concerned.
2. The Act made no distinction between founders and shareholders. Both were treated alike as members of the company, enjoying equal rights and subject to the same liabilities.
3. The Act stipulated that the first balance sheet should cover a period of no less than twelve months and prohibited the assignment or transfer of shares and debentures before that date. The Court was allowed to rule automatically null and void any earlier assignment.
4. Founders were not allowed to dispose of their shares until at least three years after the incorporation of the company. Here too, the Court

was allowed to rule null and void any breach of this rule.[8]
5. Companies offering shares for public subscription had to have minimum capital of 500,000 Rupees;[9] private companies had to have a capital base of at least 100,000 Rupees.

The Act also laid down rules for the formation, administration, winding up and final liquidation of public companies. The Act's provisions were based on established Kuwaiti custom and usage, which the companies already set up would have been observing. They also incorporated elements of company law from Arab states such as the Lebanon, Syria, Egypt and Iraq.

In the years 1960–62, following the promulgation of the Commercial Companies Act, 13 public companies were formed, with a total capital base of KD 35.8m. The state, which played an important part in the formation of these companies, invested about KD 15.4m in seven of the 13 new companies, representing 43 per cent.[10] The objects and activities of the newly-formed companies fell into three sectors: financial, industrial, and transport and services, the largest of which (in terms of number of shares and capital invested) was the financial sector, which included banks and insurance companies.

The reasons for the popularity of the financial sector, which had attracted so much more investment than the industrial sectors, was due to two factors:[11]

1. Because of the high costs involved, the return on capital invested in industry was considerably lower than capital invested in financial assets.
2. Any gains from industrial investment would only be long-term.

Investment in the financial sector had the following advantages:

1. Quick and rapidly realisable profits.
2. The possibility of rapid transfer of assets into cash.
3. Good prospects for capital gain.

As the financial market lacked a strong and sound organisational structure, and because of slack compliance with the existing regulations and the absence of any legislation designed to exclude undesirable investors, the door was wide open for investment not only by the experts but by small investors.

During its first years, the market thrived. Oil revenues were high, the government was spending lavishly on infrastructure, public amenities, roads and housing, and making generous compensation to people whose property had been affected by the new planning schemes.[12] Individual's assets were highly liquid at the time, and they entered the market in several ways. These years saw the beginning of large scale stock exchange activity and the pace increased as people with widely varying sums to invest began to deal in stocks. The period also witnessed considerable activity by speculators, which threatened the future of the market and impeded its health in the economic growth of the country. Speculation caused share prices to soar to levels quite unrelated to the companies' performance. Brokers with little knowledge of the markets, whose only experience was as estate agents, rose to prominent positions as dealers.

In the absence of any regulatory or legislative framework, the sixties saw acute fluctuations of the money market and tumbling share prices. Investors began to lose confidence, especially when companies failed to distribute dividends. With falling confidence in the quoted companies, the number of traders amounted to barely 300,[13] according to one estimate.

There was a virtual moratorium on the formation of new companies between the years 1963–69, when only eight were incorporated; this compares with nine companies incorporated between the years 1961–62.[14] Substantial shareholdings by the state of as much as 60 per cent of total authorised capital in the new companies were a measure of the reluctance of the public and private sectors to get involved.

By the end of 1968, there were 25 limited companies in Kuwait, with total nominal capital KD 100m, of which 43 per cent was owned by the government and 57 per cent by the private sector.[15] The majority of investment was now taken by the industrial sector, due to the growth of the petrochemical industries which represented Kuwait's industrial base; this was characterised by heavy capital investment and the financial sector dropped to second place.

By the beginning of the seventies, it became evident that the local market was in urgent need of new regulations that would reflect its growing size and importance. Several acts and government restrictions were brought into force to govern dealings in shares and securities, precursors to the founding of the stock exchange.

Law No. 32/1970 authorised the Minister of Trade and Industry to issue regulations governing trading in shares of Kuwaiti public companies. A Consultative Financial Commission was set up, as stipulated in Article 11, consisting of the Minister of Trade and Industry (chairman) and nine other members: two from the Ministry of Trade and Industry, a representative from the Ministry of Finance, a representative of the Central Bank and five other members of known expertise and experience. The Commission's role was as follows:[16]

1. To propose legislative and regulatory provisions with respect to the stock market.
2. To submit proposals for the creation of a stock exchange.
3. To suggest laws to safeguard the national financial and economic interest in the event of abnormal fluctuations in the prices of shares and securities.
4. To advise on the registration of any foreign firm wishing to offer shares on the Kuwaiti market.
5. To enforce laws and regulations pertaining to securities.

The Minister of Trade and Industries' Ministerial Resolution No. 10/1971,[17] issued on 8th August 1971, asked the Comptroller of Companies and Insurance to:

Compile statistical analyses of Kuwaiti public companies and of the movement of their shares and profits;
Publish an official daily bulletin of share prices thereafter;
Promote greater awareness about investment amongst the general public by the regular release of news handouts to the press, radio and television, in co-operation with the relevant authorities.

The Minister also ordered all stockbrokers to register with the Ministry of Trade and Industry and to report all share transactions and negotiations. Other Articles governed the conditions to be met by applicants for entry into the stock market brokers' register. The daily, monthly, quarterly and annual share bulletins issued by the Department of Investment and Securities within the Ministry of Trade nowadays constitute the main source of reference on the movement of shares in the Kuwaiti market.[18]

The period saw hectic movement in shares and unprecedented share price rises. Eight new property companies were formed between 1972–74 (Table 1.1), which allowed the small investor to have a stake in their profitability at a time of generally restricted investment opportunity. Property share prices rose by 250 per cent within two years of the formation of these companies, leading to heavy speculation in land and property and to over-valuation of their assets. Large numbers entered the market, backed by freely-available bank credit, which increased the number of share applications to the point that some new share

Table 1.1: Kuwaiti Public Companies 1952–80

Company	Date of foundation	Authorised capital KD*	Total number of shares
Banks			
National Bank of Kuwait	19.05.52	19,465,875	19,465,875
Kuwaiti Commercial Bank	19.06.60	18,144,000	18,144,000
Gulf Bank	23.11.60	10,080,000	10,080,000
Kuwaiti Al-Ahli Bank	23.05.67	12,000,000	12,000,000
Kuwait and Middle East Bank[1]	24.02.71	9,600,000	9,600,000
Kuwaiti Real Estate Bank	13.05.73	9,101,408	9,101,408
Bank of Bargan	27.12.75	10,000,000	10,000,000
Kuwaiti Finance House[2]	23.03.77	10,000,000	10,000,000
Investment			
Kuwaiti Investment	25.11.61	21,073,268	21,073,268
Kuwaiti Commercial, Contracting and Foreign Investments	16.01.65	25,000,000	25,000,000
Kuwait International Investments	22.09.73	15,639,000	15,639,000
Kuwait International Oil Investments	10.12.80	100,000,000	100,000,000
Insurance			
Kuwait Insurance	30.07.60	5,250,000	5,250,000
Gulf Insurance	09.04.62	4,147,200	4,147,200
Al-Ahli Insurance	12.06.62	2,700,000	2,700,000
Warba Insurance	24.10.76	4,000,000	4,000,000
Industrial			
Kuwaiti National Oil	05.10.60	15,000,000	15,000,000 **
National Industries	10.08.60	15,245,858	15,245,858
Kuwait Flour Mills	23.10.61	2,000,000	2,000,000
Petrochemicals Industry	23.07.63	32,000,000	32,000,000 **
Kuwaiti Foods (Americana)	29.12.63	2,230,800	2,230,800
Kuwaiti Metal Pipes Manufacturing	24.08.66	6,160,000	6,160,000
Kuwait Cement	09.11.68	5,000,000	5,000,000
Kuwaiti United Fisheries	07.02.72	11,000,000	11,000,000
National Motor Cars Trading and Manufacturing	16.07.73	3,600,000	3,600,000
Ship Building and Repairs	02.04.74	15,000,000	15,000,000
Gulf Cables and Electric Industries	13.04.75	3,000,000	3,000,000
Sanitary Equipment Manufacturing	13.08.75	6,750,000	6,750,000
Melamine Manufacturing	25.04.76	6,000,000	6,000,000
Kuwait Tyres	28.11.76	8,000,000	8,000,000
Kuwaiti Drug Industries	25.06.80	2,830,000	2,830,000

Table 1.1 *contd.*

Company	Date of foundation	Authorised capital KD*	Total number of shares
Transport and Communications			
Kuwaiti Oil Tankers	19.09.57	25,936,605	25,936,605
Kuwaiti Communications	20.09.62	4,000,000	4,000,000
Kuwaiti Navigation	19.01.65	21,000,000	21,000,000
Cattle Transport and Trading	28.11.73	9,842,040	9,842,040
Land Transport	16.07.77	10,000,000	10,000,000
Property			
Kuwait Real Estate	16.05.72	15,000,000	15,000,000
United Real Estate	04.04.73	23,260,000	23,260,000
National Real Estate	16.07.73	12,600,000	12,600,000
Services			
Kuwaiti Cinema	05.10.54	1,630,263	1,630,263
Kuwaiti Hotels	12.06.62	4,235,299	4,235,299
Kuwaiti Storage and Refrigeration Manufacturing	08.03.73	4,000,000	4,000,000
Kuwaiti United Poultry	06.01.79	4,000,000	4,000,000
Farm Products	26.09.76	10,000,000	10,000,000
General Warehouses	17.09.79	25,000,000	25,000,000

* Kuwaiti Dinars

** All shares were owned by the Government in 1976.

Source: 'Izz al-Dīn Marjān, Encyclopedia of Kuwaiti Commercial Legislation (Egypt: Al-Ahrām Commercial Press, 1978); Central Bank of Kuwait: Economic Survey of the Kuwaiti Economy over the Ten Years 1969–79; reports of Kuwaiti Ministry of Commerce and Industry.

1. The Kuwait and Middle East Bank replaced the British Middle East Bank which had been granted a licence in Kuwait in 1941.

2. Decree — Law No. 72/1977 (published in issue No. 1133 of *Kuwait Al Yawm*) authorised the Ministry of Awqaf and Islamic Affairs, the Ministry of Justice (Department of Palace Affairs), and the Ministry of Finance to establish a Kuwaiti Joint Stock Company under the name of Kuwaiti Finance House with a capital of KD 10m. The company was to undertake finance and other investment free of interest or usury as laid down in the Companies Articles of Association.

The number of companies increased in 1960, 1973, 1975, and 1976; in other years, no companies, or not more than one were established. This indicates that companies were not set up for genuine economic reasons but in response to share-trading booms.

issues were over-subscribed several hundred times.[19] Share values rose by 73 per cent in 1972, and by a further 50 per cent in 1973. However, most of the 1973 increase took place in the third quarter of the year.[20] One of the most spectacular innovations was the growth in futures trading, where shares were traded at market value plus a premium or margin, depending on the period for payment, the rate of price rises and the prevailing interest rate. The feature which distinguished these transactions as a form of bank credit was that the buyer could sell the shares for cash before paying the account in full, because of trust between dealers and the absence of any legal or regulatory controls.[21] By 1974, the share market was stagnant compared to the record levels it had reached in 1973. Turnover dropped from 10.5m (1973–74) to 3.9m (1974–75).[22]

Attributing the recession in part to the futures market, the Minister of Trade issued order No. 52/1974[23] in December banning the sale of futures in securities or shares until further notice. Until that point there had been increasing use of deferred payment and speculation had mounted.

In the same year, a Commission was set up under the supervision of a Planning Council, to study public companies. Given that such companies were a vehicle for channelling accumulated liquid assets into production and renewable sources of income, the Commission's role was to set guidelines for appropriate investment policies and sectorial priorities. The Commission was also to advise on the formation of new companies that would direct savings into economically productive areas, a policy which attempted to combine the social objectives of the economy with commercial profitability.

To guarantee that shares were available to the widest possible number of people, the Commission recommended that a ceiling be imposed on subscriptions, designed to enable small savers to enter the market.[24] Decree No. 3/1975 set the minimum nominal share value at KD 1,[25] as compared to KD 7.500 under the earlier Act No. 15/1960. The Commission also recommended that a study be undertaken on the body of law regulating public companies, which would put forward amendments. The preamble to law No. 3/1975 reads:

> The government has been eager to promote domestic investment and to encourage shareholding by the largest possible number and to see the benefits of shareholding enjoyed by the largest possible number of people. This honourable page of our economic activity has been tarnished by regrettable actions that run against the ethical standards that characterise authentic Kuwaiti business traditions. Whereas dealing in shares has spread to all classes of the nation, it has become imperative that controls should be introduced to safeguard shareholders and protect the benefits inherent in this important economic activity. Therefore, the accompanying Bill has been designed to close the

loopholes that have become apparent, which have been exploited for personal gain and are contradictory to the rules of good faith and honesty.[26]

Decree No. 3/1975 introduced amendments with immediate effect to provisions in law No. 15/1960 affecting commercial companies, forbidding dealings in new-company shares for at least twelve months after publication of the first balance sheet, and ordering the founder-directors to vet applications prior to the allocation of shares in order to ascertain that no offences were committed, such as subscriptions under fictitious names. The Decree also laid down penalties for offenders. The reason behind the provision was that large investors used to 'buy' the use of other people's names in order to purchase shares on their own account.[27] The more simple-minded would 'sell' their name to several people so their name would appear on more than one subscription. Another abuse was for big investors to fake names in order to obtain shares.

Organisation of the Kuwait Stock Exchange

On 2nd November 1976 the Trade and Industry Minister issued Ministerial Resolution No. 61/1976 in 25 Articles as follows:[28]

1. This Order regulates dealings in the instruments of the Kuwaiti Public Companies (*e.g.* Shares and Securities).
2. There shall be formed a Commission under the description 'Securities Commission' to regulate dealings in the instruments specified in Article 1, to supervise such dealings and to pave the way to create a Stock Exchange.
3. The Securities Commission shall discharge, within the limits laid down in the laws and regulations, all functions of such a nature as to normalise transactions in such a way as to safeguard investors' and companies' interests and shall, in particular:

I. Lay down regulating rules for the negotiations in securities to include:

a. Ways and means of dealing in securities.
b. Registration of companies whose securities are negotiable.
c. Regulation of spot and futures contracts.
d. Specification of the minimal date required to be provided

periodically by companies authorised to issue negotiable securities and issuing periodicals in that respect.
e. The determination of the unit of dealing.
f. Fixing commission rates.
g. Fixing dealing hours.
h. The provisional suspension of dealings in a given company's securities due to abnormal charges in the prices thereof or in all articles and securities should need arise and subsequent to necessary investigations.
II Consider and decide upon complaints by dealers and brokers.

III Submit recommendations to raise the standard of dealing in securities, to promote and propagate investment consciousness.

IV Submit studies to create a permanent stock exchange and suggest the necessary legislation.

4. The Securities Commission shall consist of ten members as follows:

a. Two representatives of the Trade and Industry Ministry, of which one shall be the Chairman, to be known as the Government Delegate and in the absence of whom the other representative shall replace him with all his powers.
b. A representative of the Central Bank.
c. Two representatives of the Kuwaiti Chamber of Commerce and Industry, one of whom will be a Chairman of the Board of a company whose securities are negotiable, but not being an investment company.
d. A registered stockbroker representative, to be elected by his peers.
e. A representative of investment shareholding companies incorporated by an Emiri Decree.
f. Three acknowledged experts.

5. The Chairman and Members of the Securities Commission shall be appointed and their remuneration shall be determined under an order by the Trade and Industry Minister for three years, renewable.
6. The Commission shall convene at least ten times annually, at the invitation of the Chairman.
7. The Stock Market Committee shall appoint an executive committee under the Chairmanship of the government representative and comprising three members from the main committee, one of whom

shall be a broker. Its task shall be restricted to monitoring share trading transactions and operations within the powers conferred upon it; it shall submit interim reports about its activities to the Stock Market Committee, and shall meet twice a month at least. Its decisions shall be effective after endorsement by the Ministry of Commerce and Industry.

8. A permanent arbitration committee shall be appointed from amongst members of the Stock Market Committee to look into complaints and disputes from traders and brokers referred to it.

9. The government representative shall be responsible for the implementation of decisions and recommendations by the Stock Market Committee after endorsement by the Minister of Commerce and Industry; he shall also submit proposals and studies to the committee.

10. The Securities and Investment Department of the Ministry of Commerce and Industry shall be entrusted with all executive tasks concerning share trading including the issuing of trading coupons, registration of transactions, the issuing of handouts and pamphlets, control of activities of brokers and checking their registers to verify compliance with the Department rules, control over adjustments in registers of equity partners in companies whose shares are traded in under the committee's supervision, and any other tasks deemed necessary for the implementation of decisions by the Stock Market Committee.

Figure 1.1: Structure of the Securities Commission[29]

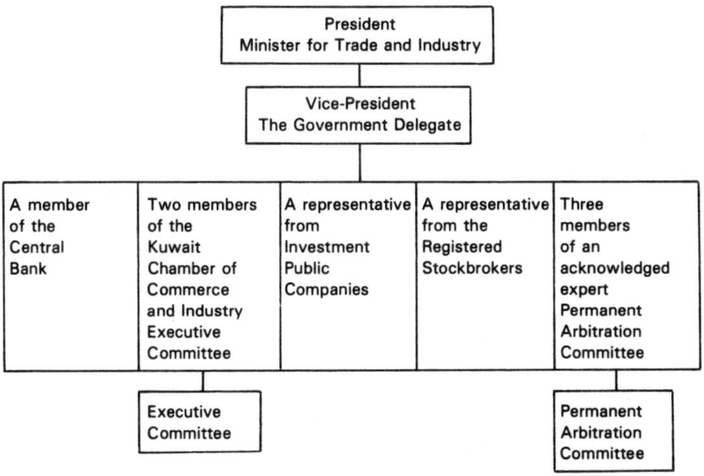

Figure 1.2: Structure of the Securities Administration[30]

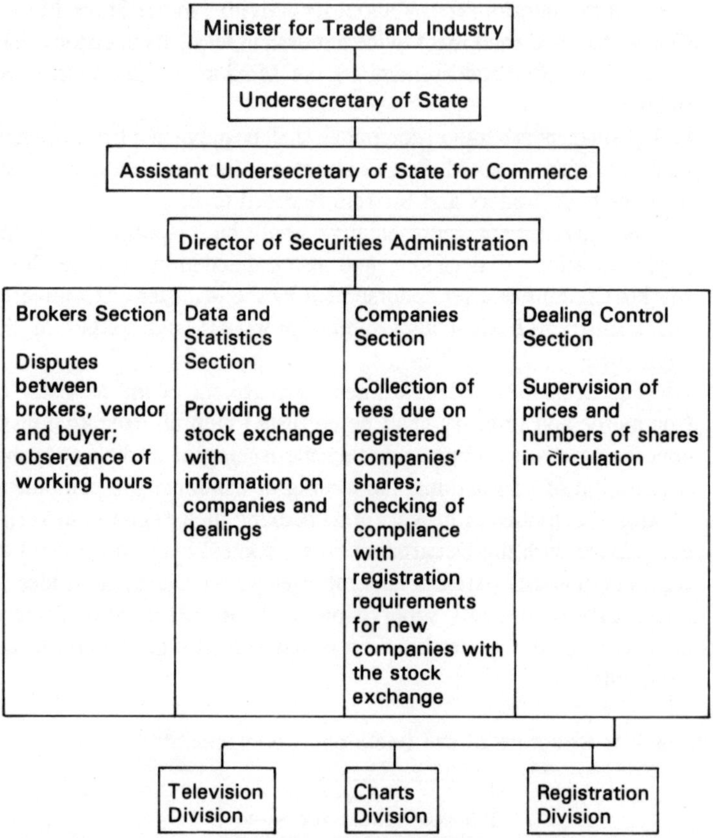

The Securities Administration acted as the Executive Authority for the Stock Exchange and consisted of four sections: brokers, data and statistics, companies, and dealing control. It had 16 members.

The role of the Securities Administration can be summarised as follows:[31]

1. To distribute books and coupons of spot and futures dealings among the brokers for a notional fee.
2. To receive and record transactions coupons from brokers.
3. To record dealings and prices on noticeboards in the Operations Hall of the Stock Exchange and to display prices on closed circuit television screens.

4. To keep records of transactions coupons, which are to be retained and used as formal documents in the event of any offence.
5. To issue daily bulletins of the quantities in circulation and the prices thereof for publication in the daily press, the bulletins to be compiled subsequently to make weekly, monthly, quarterly and annual bulletins.

The Stock Exchange and Permanent Securities Market was established on 12th April 1977, the actual date on which dealings in shares became governed by laws and regulations. Although dealings were confined to shares in Kuwaiti companies, the market occupied an impressive place in the world securities market, when the number of shares in Kuwait in 1975–76 reached 176m.[32] In 1977, business in shares dropped to 66 per cent of shares in circulation compared to 1976. The main reason for the recession in prices and circulation in 1977 lay in the rise recorded in 1976 (especially during the first half); share prices recorded an average increase of 134.7 per cent during 1976.[33]

To cope with the situation, the Security Commission lifted the ban on futures dealings in securities under Ministerial Order No. 31/1977, in an attempt to reflate the market, although it stipulated certain restrictions in respect of mode of payment, duration of the contract and its registration with the Ministry of Trade. Further measures were taken in August 1977:[34]

1. Provisional suspension of the formation of public companies (public subscription) to enable the market to absorb existing newly-formed companies. From the date of this suspension till the end of the first half of 1979, no new public companies were formed until the Public Warehouses in June 1979.
2. Increase of capital in public companies was restricted to a minimum. No public companies offered new issues in 1978; capital increases were restricted to scrip issues paid either from profits or reserves (a factor that contributed to the tumbling share prices discussed in Chapter 4). When restrictions on capital were lifted in 1979, companies rushed to launch new issues to the value of KD 27.6m, at an issue premium amounting to KD 63m, in addition to scrip issue values of about KD 31m.
3. On the Government's behalf, the Foreign Investment Corporation began buying up private sector shares at minimum market prices. This continued from December 1977 to April 1978, during which period the Government bought shares to a total value of about KD 150m.

4. A reduction in interest rates was agreed by the banks, so as to ease the financial burden on the customers; an extension of loan repayments over two years was granted by banks to finance share transactions, renewable in accordance with the circumstances of each borrower; this was so as to enable investors to retain shares rather than dispose of them at a loss. The move reduced the supply and halted the fall in prices.

The ban on the formation of new companies remained until mid 1979 when the authorities allowed the incorporation of some companies. The first was the General Warehouse Company, which was incorporated on 17th September 1979 to set up, manage and lease stores and warehouses. Trading in General Warehouse, whose capital amounted to KD 25m, began only in 1981, when the Government took up 50 per cent of the shares. The Government's stake in local companies as at 31st December 1979 amounted to KD 152,262,476 out of a combined authorised capital of KD 429,560,331 (35 per cent).[35]

The Kuwaiti Pharmaceutical Company was formed on 25th June 1980 to manufacture, produce, distribute and trade in medicines and medical appliances, with capital of KD 6m;[36] its shares were not tradeable until the end of 1980. On 10th December 1980 Offshore Kuwaiti International Company for Petrol Investments was formed, to work overseas in the petroleum refining industry, transport and storage; the Kuwait Government took 70 per cent of the KD 100m capital, and the shares were listed on the Securities Market on 25th March 1982.[37]

In spite of the lifting of the ban on the formation of new companies only three were incorporated and the Government was the largest investor. One reason may be that investors began forming companies in other Gulf States once they realised that the Kuwaiti market was saturated with Kuwaiti companies, that market prices had reached their peak and that obtaining a licence in Kuwait was not as easy as in the other Gulf States.

Impact of the Stock Exchange on the Kuwaiti Economy

The market in shares achieved a number of important economic objectives, the most significant of which are that:

It provided liquidity and diverted the risk of inflation, which had reached dangerous proportions both locally and worldwide during the seventies. Nevertheless, the role of the share market in mobilising resources, which occurs on a large scale in many countries, was not pressing in Kuwait, which faced no serious problems in the provision of funds. Traders were able to provide the finance to fund any project launched in Kuwait. Moreover, the market was particularly strong in the seventies, when some new companies had their share offers over-subscribed several times (*e.g.* Kuwait International Investment Company (136-fold), National Company for Motorcar Manufacture and Trading (109-fold), and Refrigeration Warehouses (43-fold)).[38]

Private investors sharpened their economic and investment awareness and increased their acumen in dealing with companies and businesses; this promoted the economic recovery which reached record levels during the seventies, when loans to the trade sector leapt at an annual average of 86 per cent between 1974–75.[39]

The authorities tried to direct investment throughout the economy, so as to provide each sector with companies capable of meeting the community's needs for goods and services. Their object was to broaden the industrial base of the domestic economy, create new job opportunities and channel the oil surplus into the domestic economy. Because the oil revenues were vital to the social and economic progress of the domestic economy, the authorities attempted to divert them from the risks inherent in overseas investment. Domestic companies were considered the most suitable vehicle to direct more financial resources towards investment and employment and to help in the creation of a solid economic base.

Nevertheless, as a result of the lack of legislation and regulatory framework from the outset and the absence of the necessary awareness in this field to raise the standard of individual interest, quick profit-making and unsound criteria diverted many companies from the aims for which they had been incorporated.

Figure 1.3: Movement of Share Prices. Average monthly closing prices of companies registered on the stock exchange, January 1976–April 1982.

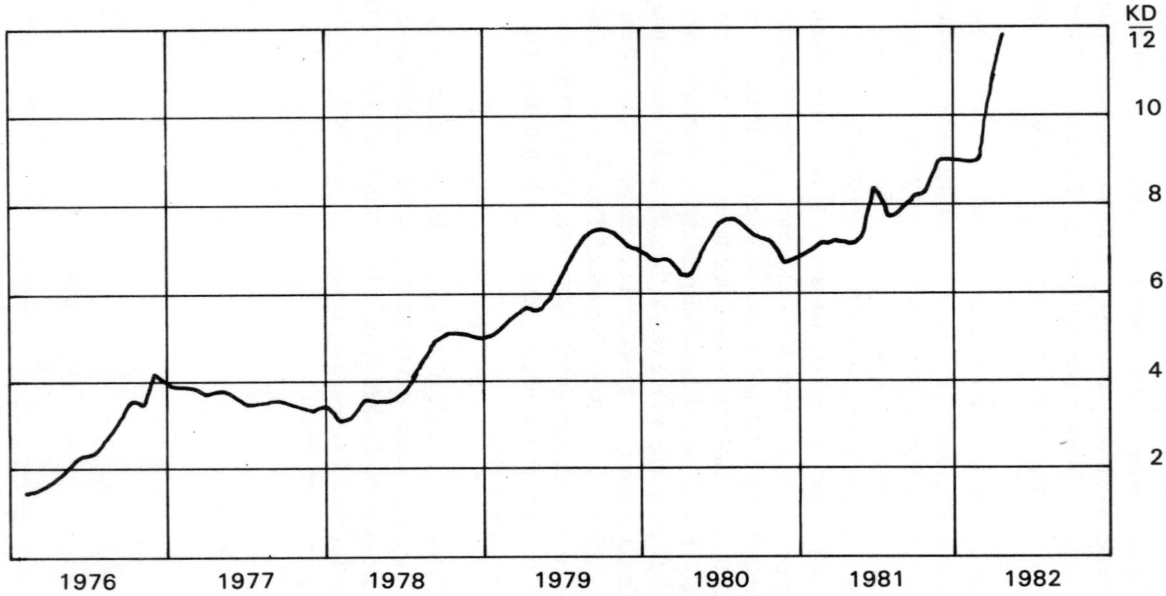

Source: *Kuwaiti Stock Exchange 1976–82* (International Kuwaiti Investment Co).
Sharp price fluctuations indicate that speculation was the overriding factor in share trading; purely economic factors tended to play no role in determining prices.

Table 1.2: Maximum and Minimum Share Prices 1976–82 (Kuwaiti Dinars)

Company	1976		1977		1978		1979		1980		1981		1982	
	Max	Min	Max	Min	Max	Min	Max	Min	Max	Min	Max	Min	Max	Min
Gulf Bank	4,910	2,180	4,360	3,150	7,810	3,860	18,800	6,280	18,820	12,620	22,320	12,650	28,500	20,160
Kuwaiti Commercial Bank	6,720	1,880	5,840	4,740	9,070	5,220	13,500	7,850	13,800	10,010	18,330	11,690	23,500	15,000
National Bank of Kuwait	3,040	1,030	3,720	3,860	8,210	3,020	20,210	7,360	19,180	12,190	22,176	13,000	28,500	20,020
Kuwait International Investments Co	3,700	0,650	2,990	1,830	2,780	1,810	3,250	2,100	4,220	2,310	6,690	2,990	9,850	6,070
Kuwait Investments Co	5,310	1,820	4,550	2,850	5,260	2,860	6,870	5,010	6,340	4,300	6,980	3,650	8,450	5,730
Gulf Insurance Co	5,890	1,410	5,890	4,530	7,240	3,980	15,650	7,090	17,710	13,880	22,140	13,390	26,500	21,790
Al-Ahli Insurance Co	4,120	1,570	3,680	3,600	8,900	3,680	15,220	8,550	14,420	12,180	18,460	11,540	21,500	17,310
Kuwait Cement	2,880	1,040	2,920	2,690	8,610	2,220	15,770	7,830	16,840	12,340	22,080	13,750	22,000	16,250
Kuwait United Fisheries Co	3,050	0,740	2,920	1,540	1,890	1,280	2,110	1,540	2,320	1,610	6,200	1,920	8,110	5,110
National Industries Co	3,920	1,360	3,750	3,700	7,730	2,510	14,480	7,030	10,510	7,130	10,960	7,130	11,250	8,700
Kuwaiti Foods Co (Americana)	0,850	0,590	1,280	0,850	1,610	0,950	4,110	1,520	7,000	3,210	7,010	4,380	7,320	5,310
Kuwait Real Estate Co	4,920	1,140	4,910	4,350	6,920	3,780	8,850	5,120	9,460	6,470	12,880	7,420	18,250	10,670
Kuwaiti Cinema Co	6,170	1,790	6,170	5,590	6,360	3,040	5,920	4,920	8,530	5,200	16,410	8,530	24,300	16,670
Kuwaiti Hotels Co	4,000	1,620	4,050	3,860	4,750	4,630	6,210	4,460	6,040	4,530	4,720	3,770	9,340	4,150

Source: *Kuwaiti Stock Exchange 1976–82* (International Kuwaiti Investment Co)

Notes

1. A.A. Bearle and G.C. Means, *The Modern Corporation and Private Property*, (New York: Harcourt, Brace & World, Inc 1932), pp. 112–16.

2. M.W. Khouja and P.G. Sadler, *The Economy of Kuwait: Development and Role in International Finance*, (London: Macmillan Press Ltd 1979).

3. Hazem El-Beblawi and Raid Fahmi, 'Role of the Stock Market in Kuwait Economy', paper submitted to the Conference on the Development of the Stock Market in Kuwait between 14th and 16th November 1981, (Kuwait: Kuwaiti Chamber of Commerce and Industry, 1981), p. 27.

4. El-Beblawi and Fahmi, 'Role of the Stock Market', p. 27.

5. Al-Khouja Muhammad and Said Walid, *Stocks of Kuwait Companies, Analytic Study*, (Kuwait: Economic Association Press, 1974).

6. 'Act No. 15/1960 promulgating, the Commercial Companies Law', (Kuwait: *Kuwait Al Yawm, Official Gazette*, No. 276, 23.5.60).

7. Amended by the Law Decree No. 3, 1975.

8. Included in Article 5 of Law Decree No. 3, 1975.

9. 1 KD = 13½ Indian Rupees, which was the prevailing currency throughout the Gulf.

10. El-Beblawi and Fahmi, 'Role of the Stock Market', p. 29.

11. Al-Khouja Muhammad, written comment on a paper submitted to the Conference on the Development of the Stock Market in Kuwait, (Kuwait: Kuwaiti Chamber of Commerce and Industry, 1981), p. 102.

12. Muhammad Al-Rumayhi, *Oil and Social Change*, (Kuwait: Al-Wahda publication and distribution corporation, 1975), p. 28.

13. 'Formation of a Kuwaiti Stock Exchange', Initial Report submitted to the Ministry of Commerce and Industry, June 1970.

14. Table 1.1: 'The Mysteries of the World of Gulf Shares Speculation in Kuwait', *Al Bayan* [Dubai: newspaper], No. 628, 4.2.82, p. 3.

15. Hazem El-Beblawi and Raid Fahmi, *The Kuwait Stock Exchange*, IBM papers, series No. 6, (Kuwait: The Industrial Bank of Kuwait KSC, January 1982), p. 29.

16. 'Act No. 32/1970 on Organisation of Trading in the Securities of Kuwaiti Shareholding Companies', *Kuwait Al Yawm*, No. 806, 1970.

17. 'Ministerial Resolution No. 10/1971, on Organisation of Kuwaiti company stocks', *Kuwait Al Yawm*, 15.8.1971.

18. Central Bank of Kuwait, *Ten Years of Kuwait's Economy*, Economic Survey 1969–79, p. 105.

19. El-Beblawi and Fahmi, IBM papers, p. 39.

20. Al-Khouja and Said, *Stocks of Kuwaiti Companies, an Analytic Study*, (Kuwait: Economic Association Press, 1974).

21. Hazem El-Beblawi, Economic Dictionary, Supplement to the Economic Bulletin, (Kuwait: Ministry of Finance, 1977).

22. *6th Annual Report*, Central Bank of Kuwait, p. 28.

23. Central Bank of Kuwait, Economic Survey, 1969–79, p. 105.

24. Ibid.

25. Article 11 of Law No. 3/1975.

26. 'Izz-al-dīn Marjān, *Encyclopedia of Kuwaiti Commercial Legislation*, (Egypt: Al-Ahrām Commercial Press, 1978), p. 91.

27. *Al Qabas* [Kuwait: newspaper], 18.5.76, p. 5.

28. 'Ministerial Resolution No. 61/1976 on Organisation of Trading in the Securities of Kuwaiti Public companies', *Kuwait Al Yawm*, No. 1108, 7.11.76.

29. Ibrāhīm al-Dharbān, 'Management of the Kuwaiti Stock Exchange', paper submitted to the Conference on the Development of the Stock Market in Kuwait, between 14th and 16th November (Kuwait: Kuwaiti Chamber of Commerce and Industry, 1981), p. 253.

30. Dharbān, 'Kuwaiti Stock Exchange', p. 253.
31. Article No. 14 in Ministerial Resolution No. 61/1976.
32. Salem Marzouq Al Tuhaih, *The Securities Market in Kuwait*, (Kuwait: Amiri Diwan, Office of Research and Consultancy to his Highness the Amir, 1983), p. 8.
33. *Annual Report*, Kuwait Ministry of Commerce and Industry, 1976, p. 36; also see table 1.2 and figure 1.3.
34. Central Bank of Kuwait, Economic Survey, 1969–79, pp. 106–8.
35. 'Awad Al-Hamūd and Rifā'ī M. Rifā'ī, 'Role of the Board in Kuwaiti Public Companies, Theory and Practice', *Journal of Gulf and Arabian Peninsula Studies*, Vol. IX, No. 35, July 1983, pub. Kuwait University, p. 51.
36. Table 1.1.
37. Share price bulletin, *Al Watan* and *Al Qabas* [Kuwait: newspapers], 26.3.82.
38. Central Bank of Kuwait, Economic Survey, 1969–79, p. 109.
39. Ibid.

2

Gulf Public Companies 1976-82

Emergence and Development

In the mid seventies, some of the Gulf States witnessed the emergence of a new type of share company based on different share structures and methods of trading. The separate *Al Manakh*[1] stock market was established for these *Khalijyat* in 1978. These companies are the subject of this chapter since, together with local Kuwaiti companies, they constituted the core of the stock market, creating its prosperity and precipitating its eventual collapse. From the legal point of view, Gulf public companies are considered joint ventures in view of the joint nature of their capital equity which is shared by persons from different sovereign states; they also perform other functions, varying from share trading and property business to industrial and agricultural investment.[2]

The emergence of these companies was the outcome of emigration from the capital by a number of Kuwaiti investors to some of the United Arab Emirates, and subsequently to Bahrain, because the neighbouring Gulf countries provided better opportunities for investment. The main developments and reasons leading to the establishment of those companies are:

1. During the seventies, when the Kuwait market was saturated, the Government imposed restrictions, such as the Kuwaiti Government decision of August 1977 to ban the establishment of new companies.[3] But these restrictions came during the period of wealth created by the fast growing oil boom in Kuwait and other Gulf countries.[4] In view of the cultural homogeneity of the Gulf peoples, the emigration of Kuwaiti investors to neighbouring Gulf countries, in the search for new investment opportunities, was natural. They were

warmly welcomed in some of these states, which saw common benefits in the proposed ventures.

2. For the ambitious Kuwaiti investor, the other Gulf countries offered attractive prospects. However, not all Gulf States welcomed them. Saudi Arabia, for instance, has laws against non-nationals,[5] similar to Kuwait's. In Kuwait, only Kuwaitis are allowed to take a stake in local companies, and only Kuwaitis may trade in their shares.[6] It was not unusual for Kuwaitis to find themselves confronted with similar laws and regulations in other Gulf States, since governments are entitled to take measures to safeguard the interests of their people. The rampant speculation in the Kuwaiti market, which had contributed to the market collapse in 1976, had made other Gulf States more cautious. However, Kuwaiti investors were welcomed in some Emirates of the UAE, and later in Bahrain, areas which needed Gulf investment to improve conditions and achieve economic development. The Emirates which issued decrees and licences for Gulf companies were either small producers or non-producers of oil, such as Sharjah, Ras Al-Khaimah, Ajman, Fujairah, Umm-Al-Qaiwain, and occasionally Dubai.[7] The establishment of Gulf public companies in the Emirates was chaotic. In Bahrain, however, where the Ministry of Commerce has sole authority, the new market was more orderly. All companies are subject to Bahrain's Commercial Companies Law (Decree No. 28, November 1975);[8] hence all applications to establish new companies are subject to careful scrutiny by the authorities.

3. The absence of federal laws to govern the activities of companies in the UAE, and the limited role of the Federal Ministry of Commerce, made it easy for Kuwaiti investors to procure licences in the UAE, and therefore to establish more and more companies — a proof of this is that the Trading Company Law in the UAE came into force in 1984.[9]

4. The passive attitude of the authorities in Kuwait towards the trading of Gulf companies in the Kuwaiti stock market persuaded Kuwaiti investors that Gulf companies could enjoy both the status of local companies in their Gulf countries of 'origin' and the benefit of being traded in the Kuwait market, which has rapid contacts with the rest of the financial world.

5. Kuwaiti investors used to the full advantages peculiar to the Gulf States. For example:

In the absence of appropriate laws and regulations, the 'legal' and contractual status of these companies depended wholly on decrees and individual company contracts and Articles of Association. Actual control over the policies and resources of the company was concentrated in Kuwaiti hands — as founders, major subscribers and owners of the majority of stock.[10]

The Gulf States were inexperienced in investment, share trading and speculation — a fact fully exploited by Kuwaiti investors, who confined share trading in the Kuwaiti stock market to the benefit of Kuwaitis especially, in view of the absence of another stock exchange in any other Gulf country.

Taking full advantage of these circumstances, which constituted an obvious attraction for Kuwaiti capital, Kuwaitis initially offered 50-50 participation with investors from the Gulf countries, but ended up acquiring 80 or even 90 per cent. Thus during the early stages of the history of these companies, subscription by local people was negligible. The Sharjah Group, for example, the first of the Gulf companies, was founded in 1976 under the Emiri Decree No. 133/76 of 16th November 1976, issued by the Ruler of Sharjah, with an authorised capital of 500m UAE Dirhams and paid up capital of 250m UAE Dirhams.[11] The company's Articles of Association reveal that the list of subscribers consists of 66 individuals and institutions; out of the total of 26,800,000 shares, only 2,600,000 were owned by just three UAE citizens.[12]

The situation reflects the care practised by Kuwaitis in those early stages not to involve a large number of non-Kuwaitis. It reflects too the extent to which non-Kuwaitis lacked both know-how and liquidity.

However, the lists of founders and subscribers of companies established later indicate that the number of local subscribers steadily increased as they came to realise the benefits involved: for example, the Gulf Financial Centre established under Emiri Decree No. 57/1979, issued on 8.9.79, and the Sharjah Cement and Industrial Development Company, established under Emiri Decree No. 31/79, issued on 12.5.79.[13] People started to compete to acquire stakes having tasted the large and quickly-obtained profits.

The Gulf public companies constituted a meeting point between Kuwaiti investors and those of other Gulf States. These companies acquired the dual status of being 'Gulf' by virtue of birth and nationality, and Kuwaiti by virtue of structure. Despite their illegal status in Kuwaiti law, trading in their shares in the parallel stock exchange surpassed that of the legally-recognised indigenous Kuwaiti companies.

The first companies to emerge as the Gulf market started in the mid-seventies, were the Sharjah Group, established in Sharjah in 1976 by an Emiri Decree, and the United Insurance Company, established in Ras Al-Khaimah in the same year.

Starting with relatively large capital and financially well-established shareholders, the Sharjah Group had broad-ranging objectives:[14]

1. To undertake all activities pertaining to investment, industry and research relevant to the employment of capital, and to offer all services connected with such activities.
2. To establish companies and trade in their stocks and shares.
3. To invest in commercial, industrial and tourism projects.
4. To invest in property and be active in the money markets and stock exchanges.
5. To carry out international trade operations.

It is obvious that the founders of the Sharjah Group were intent (and probably still are) on establishing more companies, and on taking a stake in existing and potential companies. As a result the Sharjah Group realised large profits by acquiring a major stake in several companies. Its net profits for the year 1981 amounted to Drh. 60m compared to Drh. 19m in 1980, a difference of 206 per cent.[15]

The second of the Gulf public companies to emerge, the United Insurance Company, was relatively small. Its authorised capital was 20m UAE Dirhams, only half of it paid up,[16] since insurance companies do not need a large capital base at the outset. Taking a stake in the company together with a group of Kuwaiti investors were the Governments of Abu Dhabi and Ras Al-Khaimah.

Thereafter, Gulf shareholding companies were established in quick succession. The phenomenon is attributed to the 'fever' of share trading at the Kuwaiti Stock Exchange. Quick profits at fabulous rates seemed to attract everybody.

Kuwaiti investors forwarded applications *en masse* to establish companies, with no serious plans for any authentic purpose for the company, in the knowledge that investors at the stock exchange would not bother to ask. Delegations of Kuwaiti businessmen and investors travelled continually to the UAE and Bahrain, and sometimes Oman and Qatar, where they were warmly welcomed, and soon deals and agreements materialised. Banks in these countries opened their doors wide in the hope of attracting the value of share subscriptions or the capital of a newly formed company as deposits. Kuwaiti businessmen capitalised on the situation by applying for — and getting — loans and other bank facilities: for example, from the First Gulf Bank in Ajman, and Arab

Sahil Bank in Ras Al-Khaimah. Many Kuwaitis also approached those in power to obtain licences to establish industrial, property and other projects, without any real idea of the nature of the venture they were proposing:[17] for example, the Mining and Industries Company in Ajman, Gulf Animal Resources of Ajman, and the Ras Al-Khaimah Gulf Gas Exploitation Company. Easy profits, rather than the preliminary viability of a scheme or its contribution to the national economy, spurred them on.

Authorities in some Emirates of the UAE and in Bahrain believed that by issuing more and more licences for Gulf companies, they were contributing to prosperity and industrial development.

Four Gulf Companies

Only a year after the establishment of the first two Gulf shareholding companies, the formation of four more multi-purpose companies was announced in 1977.

1. Gulf Agriculture Development Company, established under Emiri Decree No. 105/1977, issued by the Ruler of Sharjah on 2nd June 1977. Under section 3 of the decree, authorised capital was fixed at 200m UAE Dirhams, and paid-up capital at 25 per cent of authorised capital; the remainder was to be paid according to the Articles of Association.[18] The amount of paid-up capital was increased gradually while the share price was adjusted downwards from 10 Dirhams to 2.5 Dirhams. By 1982 paid-up capital matched authorised capital at 200m Dirhams[19] and the share price was adjusted downwards again, to one Dirham.

The company's interests included agricultural activities, livestock breeding, poultry farms, fodder processing factories, ownership of a fishing fleet, and dealing in all types of agricultural equipment. Holding equity in other companies, trading in the shares of agricultural and other companies and property investment — common factors among Gulf companies — were added to the list.

Once the company was formed a provisional board of directors was drawn up. Out of the six, only one was a UAE citizen, the rest were Kuwaitis.[20] The company did not exclude citizens of any of the Gulf States from the right to hold shares; according to section 10 of the Articles of Association, 'Subscription in the company shares shall be open to all Arab citizens'.

2. *Gulf Investment and Real Estate Company,* established under Emiri Decree No. 2/1977, issued by the Ruler of Ajman on 12th January 1977. Under section 5 of the Articles of Association, authorised capital was fixed at 300m UAE Dirhams, to be distributed through 30 million shares of 10 Dirhams each. Section 7 stipulated that 25 per cent of the authorised capital was to be paid up, the remainder to be paid within five years of the date of the decree.[21]

In practice, the amount paid up stood at 75m Dirhams, and the number of shares remained unchanged at 30 million. Every shareholder was indebted to the company for 75 per cent of the value of each share, which amounted to 7.5 Dirhams to be paid over five years in a manner to be decided by the board of directors. In other words, the founders of the company decided against the immediate payment of the entire capital, while retaining the full number of shares. When the company went into profit in 1978–79 and its share value began to increase, the founders decided to increase the number of shares. To achieve this indirectly, the share value was cut from 10 Dirhams to 3 Dirhams in 1980, so that shareholders would not be required to repay the 75 per cent of the old value already registered as due to the company. Following that, the board of directors decided to issue new shares at a face value of three Dirhams, so the total number of shares swelled by 70 per cent to 100 millions in 1981 compared to 1977, the year of foundation.

In 1982 — the year when share trading peaked, heralding the big crash later in the year — the share price was slashed to just one Dirham and the number of shares traded in the market jumped by 200 per cent.[22] This additional benefit enabled shareholders to procure more shares without laying out more money. The theory was that any fall in the share value would be only temporary, after which traders would tend to forget that this new 'share' was actually a fraction of the original share. The new shares would acquire the status of the full original shares and their price would begin to rise.

The board of directors doubled the company's capital from 300m UAE Dirhams to 600m Dirhams, and as a result 300m new shares were offered for sale (one of the factors leading to the deterioration of the market was share dumping in this manner). Free bonus shares were distributed at the rate of 33.33 per cent among shareholders at the end of 1981, and new shares were issued at the rate of 66.66 per cent. Total capital in 1982 amounted to 600m Dirhams against 600 million shares with a face value of one Dirham.[23]

Section 5 of the Articles of Association defined the company's purposes so as to include undertaking industrial projects, investment in property, contracting, general commerce, hotels and restaurant construction, share trading and setting up new companies. This multiplicity of purpose is typical of Gulf public companies, particularly the share trading which proved to be fundamental, since the fabulous profits realised during the boom virtually disappeared in 1983. As this was the only year in which no share trading took place, this perhaps explains why some companies did not publish budgets, while those published reflect losses (Table 2.3).

3. Gulf Industries Company, established under Emiri Decree No. 133/1977, issued by the Ruler of Sharjah on 29th June 1977. Under section 3 of the decree, authorised capital was fixed at 120m Dirhams, and paid-up capital was fixed at 25 per cent of authorised capital. Section 2 of the decree specified the purposes of the company as follows:[24]

- i Establishment of various types of industrial plant, particularly for chrome, glass, plastics, floor carpeting, lime blocks and prefabricated buildings.
- ii Grading plant products inside and outside the UAE, and marketing them internationally.
- iii Importation and acquisition of all relevant equipment and instruments, as well as the importation of raw materials.
- iv Acquisition of land and property necessary for new installations.

Section 3 laid down that the founders would subscribe 10,200,000 shares out of a total of 12,000,000 shares, the remainder to be offered to nationals for public subscription — 85 per cent for the founders, 15 per cent for the public. The founders later bought up some of this small percentage for their families. Why did they refrain from acquiring the lot, so as to achieve 100 per cent ownership and make it a closed company? By allotting a small percentage of the shares for public subscription, the company became public, and its shares traded.

Para 3 of section 3 had stipulated that, 'Subscription in the shares of the company shall be open to nationals of the UAE, Kuwait and the Sultanate of Oman'.[25] As seen above, the only subscriptions open to nationals of the Gulf States were, apart from the UAE and Kuwait, those taken up in Oman.

4. Gulf Cement Company, established under Emiri Decree No. 24/1977, issued on 31st Mary 1977. Authorised capital was 300m Dirhams, divided into 30 million shares at a face value of 10 Dirhams each. Paid-up capital was to be 50 per cent of authorised capital. Founders subscribed 21 million shares, or 70 per cent of the total, with 9 million shares left for public subscription. Section 3 of the Decree stipulated that only UAE and Kuwait nationals were entitled to subscribe.[26]

Section 4 specified the purposes of the company as follows:

i Undertaking all types of activity relevant to the production of all grades of cement.
ii The purchase, installation and management of plants.
iii Acquiring, renting or otherwise using land.
iv Utilisation of and trading in all cement industry by-products.
v Investment of any of the company's property, whether by direct investment or collateral, in any manner the company might deem suitable; the company was also permitted to sell, replace or dispose of property.
vi All business deemed to improve the company's resources.
vii To undertake, generally, any commercial or other business deemed necessary for the interests or purposes of the company, and to invest the company money in a manner to be decided by the board of directors.

Sections v, vi and vii were far removed from the originally-stated purposes of the company, as being an industrial company specialising in the production of cement. Cement production is undoubtedly a vital industry, but it seems that the company founders were intent on profit-making, by any means, relevant or otherwise to this industry, as clearly reflected by paragraph (v) ('investment of any of the company's property . . . in any manner . . .'). Founders of Gulf public companies would deliberately seek to include such paragraphs to provide outlets for trading in shares, property speculation or taking equity in other companies, not necessarily with similar purposes.

The Gulf Cement Company did not differ from other Gulf shareholding companies in its subscription structure. Of 183 individuals and companies in the list of founders who subscribed in 21 million shares, only two were nationals of the licence-granting Emirate: Ras Al-Khaimah — 7,500,000 shares, and Khalid Al-Qasimi and Company — 1,500,000 shares. The 181 founders were from Kuwait and took 12 million shares, later acquiring most of the nine million shares offered for public subscription.[27]

As was the case with other Gulf public companies, capital was stepped

Table 2.1: Gulf Public Companies 1976–82

Company	Domicile	Date of incorporation	Authorised capital* (million)		Paid-up capital* (million)		Remarks
Investment							
Sharjah Group	Sharjah	1976	Dh	500	Dh	250	
Gulf Investment and Real Estate	Ajman	1977	"	300	"	75	
Kuwait and Gulf Financial Centre	Ajman	1979	"	240	"	120	
Gulf Real Estate	Ajman	1979	"	300	"	300	
Gulf Financial Centre	Sharjah	1979	"	200	"	200	
Ras Al-Khaimah Investment	Ras Al-Khaimah	1979	"	500	"	500	Liquidated in 1981
Coast Investment and Development	Ras Al-Khaimah	1980	"	80	"	80	
Arab Company for General Investments (Shua'a)	Dubai	1979	"	700	"	175	
Pearl Investment	Bahrain	1979	US$	75	US$	23	
Arab Development Company	Bahrain	1979	BD	10	BD	10	
Gulf Investments	Bahrain	1980	US$	250	US$	125	
Al-Jazira Contracting and Investment	Bahrain	1978	"	53	"	13	
Bahrain International Investment Centre	Bahrain	1981	"	300	"	125	95% Kuwaiti participation
Bahrain and Kuwait Investment Group (formerly Dubai Group)	Bahrain	1982	BD	55	BD	55	Registered in Dubai; did not function and licence cancelled; later registered in Bahrain
Industrial							
The Gulf Agriculture Development Company	Sharjah	1977	Dh	200	Dh	50	
Gulf Industries Company	Sharjah	1977	"	120	"	30	

Table 2.1 contd.

Company	Domicile	Date of incorporation	Authorised capital* (million)		Paid-up capital* (million)		Remarks
Sharjah Cement and Industrial Development	Sharjah	1979	Dh	150	Dh	150	
Gulf Medical Projects	Sharjah	1979	"	75	"	75	
Oriental Company for Production and Distribution	Sharjah	1979	"	60	"	30	
United International Hotels	Sharjah	1979	"	100	"	100	
Gulf Cement	Ras Al-Khaimah	1977	"	300	"	150	
Ras Al-Khaimah Company for White Cement & Construction Materials Industry	Ras Al-Khaimah	1980	"	600	"	600	
Gulf Drug Industries	Ras Al-Khaimah	1980	"	100	"	100	
Ras Al-Khaimah Poultry and Fodder	Ras Al-Khaimah	1981	"	40	"	40	
Gulf Kalankar	Ras Al-Khaimah	1982	US$	350	US$	175	
Gulf Livestock	Ras Al-Khaimah	1982	Dh	400	Dh	200	Shares not traded in *Manakh*
Mining and Industry	Ajman	1979	"	200	"	70	
Ajman Cement	Ajman	1980	"	225	"	225	
Gulf Industrial and Real Estate	Ajman	1980	"	100	"	100	
Petroleum Products	Ajman	1981	"	400	"	200	
Gulf Animal Resources	Ajman	1982	Dh	200	Dh	200	Shares not traded in *Manakh*
Fujairah Cement	Fujairah	1979	"	350	"	225	
Emirates Kalankar	Fujairah	1981	"	200	"	50	Being amalgamated with Fujairah Cement
Umm Al-Qaiwain Cement	Umm Al-Qaiwain	1982	"	500	"	500	

Table 2.1 contd.

Company	Domicile	Date of incorporation	Authorised capital* (million)		Paid-up capital* (million)		Remarks
Gulf Gas Exploitation	Umm Al-Qaiwain	1981	Dh	200	Dh	200	Shares not traded in *Manakh*
Arab Company for Iron and Steel	Bahrain	1980	US$	150	US$	150	
United Gulf Industry and Services	Bahrain	1980	"	150	"	150	
Gulf Group for Projects and Industry	Ajman	1981	"	100	"	100	
Insurance							
United Insurance	Ras Al-Khaimah	1976	Dh	20	Dh	10	
Gulf Union Insurance	Bahrain	1980	BD	8	BD	3	
Arab International Insurance	Bahrain	1980	US$	10	US$	6	
International Insurance	Ajman	1979	Dh	20	Dh	20	
Sharjah Insurance and Re-assurance	Sharjah	1979	"	50	"	50	Founded as a local company in 1970 before conversion to Pan Gulf
Banks							
First Gulf Bank	Ajman	1979	Dh	120	Dh	120	
Arab Sahil Bank	Ras Al-Khaimah	1981	"	100	"	50	
United Gulf Bank	Bahrain	1980	US$	250	US$	75	
Bahrain and Middle East Bank	Bahrain	1981	"	500	"	100	
Bahrain International Bank	Bahrain	1982	"	300	"	180	
Arabian Investment Banking Corporation	Bahrain	1982	"	500	"	50	

* Authorised and paid-up capital figures are for the year of foundation.
Source: Company Decrees, Articles of Association and Annual Reports; *Exempted Public Companies in Bahrain*, Department of Commerce and Companies Affairs, Ministry of Commerce and Agriculture; Public Companies in United Arab Emirates, Federation of the UAE Chambers of Commerce and Industry.

up, in order to allow the acquisition of the maximum number of shares, from 300m Dirhams to 800m Dirhams[28] (Emiri Decree No. 10/1981), and the share value was cut to one Dirham, which automatically increased the number of shares to 800 million. The Articles of Association are similar to those of other Gulf companies.

After 1977 the formation of Gulf share companies continued but the emphasis shifted to Bahrain. While 1978 saw the incorporation of only one company — Al-Jazira Contracting Company, licensed in Bahrain — 1979 was a high point: about 12 companies were incorporated in that year either in the UAE or Bahrain (Table 2.1); the pace continued through to 1982 and subsided only a few months before the big crash in Kuwait.

Characteristics of Gulf Public Companies

In a relatively short number of years, Gulf public companies had become a reality in the economic life of the area. By proving their worth in the arena of the Kuwait Stock Exchange, they attracted people from all walks of life. Compared to other types of joint-stock companies in the Gulf States, Gulf public companies have certain unique characteristics:

1. As a rule Gulf public companies did not confine themselves to their original purposes. Additional purposes were always included in the Articles of Association. Gulf public companies became multi-purpose investment institutions in a variety of sectors including commerce, industry and agriculture as well as in property and shares speculation. 'Any other activities' or a similarly loosely-worded clause was always inserted by the founders to enable them to pursue other potentially profitable activities without restriction.

Because there is no body of comprehensive company law in some of the licence-granting Gulf States, founders of a Gulf company had to draw on the Articles of Association of existing companies. In some cases, these were adopted outright, with omissions and additions here and there to suit the objectives of the new founders.

2. Gulf companies were the only investment institutions in Gulf States which attracted both the wealthy and the more limited income groups. Share prices of one UAE Dirham (as specified in Articles of Association) were relatively low, whereas one share in a Kuwaiti company, for example, would be a minimum of one Kuwaiti Dinar (12.5 UAE Dirhams). This explains why trading in the shares of Gulf companies attracted people from a whole range of income groups,

so that even those with small salaries could trade in shares as a means of improving their lot.[29]

3. There was no precondition for a minimum number of shares before one could trade in Gulf companies, an almost universally accepted practice in world stock markets; even the Kuwait Stock Exchange forbids share trading by anyone who owns fewer than 1,000 shares.[30] Such restrictions unknown in the Al-Manakh Market where Gulf company shares were traded. A person was allowed to trade with only one share. This is why Al-Manakh attracted almost unprecedented speculation.

4. In many countries, founders of public companies are not allowed to sell their shares before the expiry of a stated period, dated from the time of incorporation or its opening for business. In countries like Kuwait for example, the period is fixed at three years; twelve months is the minimum.[31] This restrictive system did not apply to Gulf companies; and since there were no laws governing such companies in the licence-granting Gulf States and Emirates, contracts and Articles of Association constituted the only contractual and legal base. It was normal practice for founders of some Gulf companies to sell their shares immediately or shortly after the signature of the licensing decree — which could weaken the company and deflect it from its objectives.

5. Most Gulf companies established in the early years permitted 'any Arab citizen' to subscribe in its shares. A section to this effect was included in the Articles of Association of the first Gulf companies, such as the Sharjah Group and the Gulf Agriculture Development Company. The early founders may have wanted to utilise the savings of the maximum number of Arabs by broadening the subscription base. When the companies entered the period of boom and highly-geared profitability, restrictions were imposed so that subscription was confined to citizens of Arab Gulf States. For example, the Article of Association No. 5 of the Gulf Medical Projects Company reads: 'Subscription in the shares of the company shall be restricted to the citizens of the following States: United Arab Emirates, Kuwait, Saudi Arabia, Bahrain, Qatar and Oman.'[32] Other Gulf companies confined subscription to people of the licence-granting state and Kuwait, to the exclusion of the other Gulf States. For instance, section 10 of the Articles of Association of the Gulf Investment and Real Estate Company reads: 'Subscription in the shares of the company shall be restricted to the nationals of the United Arab Emirates and Kuwait.'[33]

6. Some Kuwaiti founders tended to consider the Gulf public companies they set up as their private property. Thus they would take

special care to include in the Articles of Association a section or sections designed to give them a majority on the board of directors. For example, section 7 of the Articles of Association of the Kuwait and Gulf Financial Company incorporated in Ajman under Emiri Decree in 1979 stipulates that seven members of the board of directors should be Kuwaiti nationals, three UAE nationals, and that the Chairman had to be a Kuwaiti.[34] This should not be surprising in the absence of company law in the UAE or other laws to govern Gulf public companies. The logical practice is for members of the board of directors to be elected by the annual general meeting. However, with the growing participation of individuals and Government institutions in 50 per cent of the equity, an Emirate Ruler would sometimes appoint a national as board chairman, and a number of nationals as board members to sit with the Kuwaiti members.

7. The fact that founders considered their companies no more than share-trading enterprises, tended to make them obsessed with publicity. Accordingly they would look for influential names to appear on the list of founders, which went to the press for publication. This was thought to give the company a better image in the eyes of prospective traders.[35] In other cases, existing Gulf companies were invited to take a stake in a newly-formed company. As mentioned above, Articles of Association of Gulf companies usually included a clause providing for the 'establishment of companies, participation in their equity or the freedom to acquire and trade in their shares'. As founders took care to include this clause and pursue it earnestly, the Gulf companies became entangled with one another;[36] consequently when the big crash came, all companies were affected simultaneously, since losses incurred by one company automatically affected others.

8. Although Gulf companies were initiated and founded in Gulf States other than Kuwait, their main offices were established in Kuwait, with branch offices operating in the UAE and Bahrain to arrange transfers of share cards between buyer and seller. Some industrial companies held their reserves outside the licence-giving state. These would be re-invested in fixed assets such as factories and factory equipment in the country of operation. Other companies used the proximity of the Kuwaiti financial markets to re-invest their reserves. Even the accounts were usually audited by Kuwait-based accountants.[37]

9. Invariably Gulf share companies paid minimum attention to their original purpose, concentrating on share trading, speculation and company information. Many consisted of nothing more than names and share trading certificates. These companies would continue in the market

for years without achieving any of their stated objectives, be they industrial, agricultural or otherwise. The exceptions include Sharjah Cement, Gulf Cement, Gulf Agriculture Development, the Sharjah Group, Fujairah Cement, and some insurance companies. But there are companies founded years ago whose plant is still in the planning stage or under construction. These include the Mining and Industry Company, Ajman Cement, Emirates Kalankar, Gulf Kalankar, Gulf Gas Exploitation, Gulf Animal Resources, and Gulf Livestock. Some of these companies may never implement their projects, because they have already directed their resources into speculation. As a result of the 1982 crash, they sustained heavy losses and a great portion of their capital was lost.

10. Participation in Gulf companies was not confined to individuals and companies; licence-granting Governments participated in varying proportions, depending on the importance of the company, Kuwait, however, invariably reserved a 50 per cent share for itself.[38] For example, the Governments of Abu Dhabi and Sharjah took equity in Sharjah Cement Development; the Government of Abu Dhabi also participated in Ras al-Khaimah and Fujairah Cement. In rare cases, other Arab governments took a stake, such as the participation of the Government of Iraq in General Corporation for Drugs and Medical Equipment. There were also some Saudi and Qatar interests.

11. Where a company was incorporated could affect its success and the stability of its shares. For instance, a company founded in a relatively large and rich Emirate had a better chance of being recognised as reputable by the market than one founded in a smaller and less prosperous Emirate. A company founded in an Emirate that strictly watched over the issuing of licences stood a better chance of attracting subscribers; and a company founded in Bahrain had a better name than one founded in any other Emirate, in view of the stricter regulations in Bahrain.

12. Fast capital growth was a striking phenomenon, as founders and shareholders tended to view this as a method for automatically increasing the number of shares.[39] This is because the difference between the face value of a new share and the already soaring market price constituted net profit. In other cases, companies would discover that, owing to the haste with which they were founded, operating costs had not been properly calculated and the need for more money compelled founders to resort to increasing paid-up capital (see Table 2.2, which shows differential percentages between the face and market value of shares).

13. Some companies derived greater prestige than others in the stock market from the names of their founders. Factors such as company

Table 2.2: Differentials Between Face and Market Values of Shares in Gulf Public Companies Traded on the Al-Manakh Stock Market in Kuwait

Company	Share face value (nominated currency unit)	Value-equivalent (Kuwaiti Fils)	Market value (Kuwaiti Fils)	Differential percentage (+)
Gulf Agriculture Development	Dh 1	80	600	650%
Sharjah Group	US$ 0.25	75	545	626%
Pearl Investment	US$ 1	300	2,850	850%
Gulf Financial Centre	US$ 0.25	75	340	353%
Fujairah Cement	Dh 1	80	615	668%
Medical Projects	Dh 1	80	450	462%
Petroleum Products	Dh 1	80	200	150%
Ras al-Khaimah Poultry and Fodder	Dh 1	80	220	175%
Al Jazira Contracting and Investment	US$ 1	300	1,700	466%
Mining and Industry	Dh 1	80	300	275%
The Coast Development and Investment	US$ 0.25	75	350	366%
First Gulf Bank	Dh 10	800	2,000	150%
Bahrain and Middle East Bank	US$ 0.50	150	750	400%
Umm Al-Qaiwain	Dh 1	80	235	193%
Gulf Real Estate	Dh 1	80	245	206%
Gulf Investments and Real Estate	Dh 1	80	430	437%
Sharjah Cement	Dh 1	80	420	425%
International Hotels	Dh 1	80	315	293%
Bahrain and Kuwait Group	Dh 1	80	400	400%
Kuwait and Gulf Financial Centre	Dh 1	80	340	325%

Note: 1 Kuwaiti Dinar = 1,000 Kuwaiti Fils
Source: Press bulletins in *Al Qabas* Daily (Kuwait), *Al Watan* Daily (Kuwait) and *Al Khaleej* Daily (UAE) on a given day in March 1982.

domicile, names of the founders and members of the Board of Directors could play a decisive role in the strength or weakness of a given share. The personality-name was so vital that in some cases it replaced the commercial name of the company in the stock market, particularly in vocal calls by dealers, preparation of contracts, or share price lists in newspapers. For example, Gulf Financial Centre (an investment company founded in 1979 by Sharjah) was popularly known in the market as *Al-Muzayni* — Yusuf al-Muzayni was one of the company's founders, owner of the largest equity share and its chairman. Kuwait and Gulf Financial Centre (an investment company founded in Ajman in 1979) was known as *Abu Khamsin*, in reference to Jawad Abu Khamsin, one of the founders and creators of the company; at other times, it was known as *Al-Muraykiz*, meaning 'the small centre', an allusion to the size of the company's capital and operations as compared to Gulf Financial Centre.

14. Dealers were another vital factor for the prosperity of a company. They could not afford not to take the choice and appointment of a dealer lightly. The dealer was the link between the company and the al-Manakh stock market. As the man in charge of the company office there, he was assumed to know the ins and outs of the market and be in a position to influence the prices of traded shares up or down. Company founders made every effort to maintain strong relationships with them, in the correct belief that they were the best medium of communication between speculators, investors and share traders.[40]

15. Borrowing by board members was also a prominent phenomenon of Gulf shareholding companies. In recent years particularly, companies have been founded with the ease of starting a grocery shop. A licensing decree was procured, Articles of Association drawn up, and paid-up capital established — yet no commercial activity was seriously entertained other than share trading. Because many companies committed themselves to operations involving sums running into the hundred millions of local currency, some founders and directors borrowed up to 100–200m Dirhams, using the company as security. The borrower would undertake to repay the money within a year or less, at interest rates as high as 40 per cent. This secret practice was exposed by the market crash in Kuwait. Some borrowers were unable to repay and companies faced bankruptcy. For example, in 1982, Yusuf 'Abd al-'Aziz al-Muzayni secured a loan of 100m Dirhams from Umm Al-Qaiwain Gas Company, of which he was a board member, to be repaid over one year at 40 per cent interest. In the following year, Muzayni repaid both principal and interest. But another Kuwaiti, 'Abd al-Jalil Bahbahānī, deputy chairman

of Gulf Animal Resources (incorporated in Ajman early in 1982 with fully paid up capital of 230m Dirhams) received from the company and with the consent of its board, 215m Dirhams to invest on its behalf. He later handed back 27m Dirhams and remained indebted by 188m Dirhams, which he refused to return, alleging that he had sustained a loss on the investment. The company brought an action against him, and an Ajman Court declared Bahbahānī was obliged to pay the company 278m Dirhams, which included an additional 90m Dirhams representing interest and fees (verdict dated 19.6.84).[41] The defendant appealed to a higher court in Sharjah which upheld the verdict. This was officially communicated to the judicial authorities in Kuwait for execution, in accordance with the bilateral judicial cooperation agreement.[42] The practice was contrary to universally accepted norms adhered to by public companies, since board members are expected in such cases strictly to observe the responsibility entrusted to them by the shareholders, in the expectation that such funds are channelled in the directions stipulated by the Articles of Association.

16. Conscious of the interlocking interests of Gulf companies and the founders' practice of extracting considerable benefits from their position, some founders combined five or six directorships, whether the companies concerned were in industry, finance or investment, since there was no law prohibiting multiple board membership.[43]

17. Founders in most companies usually owned up to 70 or 80 per cent of the total number of shares — never less than 50 per cent. This guaranteed a strong hold over board and policies and allowed them to direct the company in their own interests. Examination of Articles of Association reveals that the subscription percentage allotted to local citizens was invariably negligible compared to the percentage allotted to the founders. For example: shares allotted to nationals in United Insurance constituted 18 per cent; in Sharjah Cement and Industrial Development 10 per cent; the Gulf Financial Centre Company 25 per cent; Sharjah Group 46 per cent; Gulf Agriculture Development zero per cent; Mining and Industry 26 per cent; and Gulf Investment and Real Estate, about 33 per cent.[44]

18. Some Gulf companies, particularly those seeking to further their interests outside the region, would quote US Dollar values for their shares. Another reason for quoting in the internationally-accepted currency was to open subscription and trading to as large a number of Kuwaitis as possible.[45] Another device was to divide shares into smaller units at a lower price; the additional shares were distributed to shareholders, later up-graded into dollars, and split again the following

year into four US 25 cent units. The practice was intended to benefit shareholders and attract investors seeking low-priced shares.[46]

19. Fees were often imposed arbitrarily. Issue allowances, for example, varied between 1 per cent, 5 per cent and 10 per cent.[47] Money collected from public companies was used to cover establishment expenses and, sometimes, the cost of the free shares granted to the licensing government. Moreover, some founders were allotted free shares, some sold at a price higher than the reference price, then repaid the company from the profit — acquiring the remainder, in effect, free of charge.

Table 2.2 shows the differentials between face and market values of Gulf shares traded in al-Manakh on a given day in March 1982. The figures demonstrate the net profit enjoyed by shareholders through the differences between face value and the already soaring market price. For example, the face value of a Gulf Agriculture Development Company share was 80 Fils but the share price in the market in March 1982 was nearly 600 Fils, which created a differential between face and market value of 750 per cent, yielding a net profit to shareholders of 520 Fils. This was the case for most Gulf companies, where share prices in the market reached economically unjustifiable levels.

The absence of laws and regulations governing these companies made it possible for them to commit whatever excesses suited their interests, and in the process, to create and adopt hitherto unheard-of economic practices. However the tempo of economic development in the Gulf States was too rapid. Uncertainty and chaos was inevitable. Priorities were confused, so that it was difficult to distinguish primary objectives from secondary goals. Because of the abundance of wealth, it took time to discover the negative aspects of development, and a severe shock before the harsh reality was revealed.

The core of our study is to consider the 'Big Crash' shock, its aftermath and implications, through an analysis of the fate of Gulf companies afterwards. The study goes into the origins of the unprecedented wealth as well as the ensuing chaos and devastation both to individuals and institutions. Chapter 4 follows collapse of the stock market, which was once regarded as beyond threat.

Achievements of Gulf Companies

The number of Gulf public companies totalled 49 in 1982. Most originated in the UAE, the rest in Bahrain. No Gulf company was founded in 1982 — it was the year of the big crash of the stock market, which took place during the second half of 1982.

Gulf public companies can be classified into three categories according to the nature of their activities.

Investment Companies and Banks

The investment sector is the most heavily represented. This is probably because these companies were simple to launch and easy to run compared to companies in the industrial and agricultural sectors.

There were 17 companies in investment, of which six were banks: two in the UAE and four in Bahrain.[48] Some of these companies were successful because of the competence and experience of the founders. The Sharjah Group and Gulf Investment and Real Estate were the largest and oldest.

The Sharjah Group established itself immediately in the field of investment, opening a branch office in London in addition to offices in Sharjah and Kuwait. It was particularly strong in property and land, investment and management portfolios, mining and industry. The Sharjah Group also acquired a stake in a Sharjah tiles production project. The company's was most active in Kuwait, where it made extensive profits by taking advantage of the investment and financing opportunities presented by the Kuwaiti capital market.

The Sharjah London office looked for openings in credit services, the management of short and long-term investments, all types of property investment and in company financing. The company took equity in numerous companies and projects in the Gulf region and the Arab world, investing altogether 67m Dirhams. In 1978, it had 30 per cent in agricultural enterprises; 26 per cent in contracting; 22 per cent in banking; 11 per cent in industry; 7 per cent in property and 4 per cent in services.[49] On top of this was the company's major presence on the Kuwait Stock Exchange, where it commanded large portfolios. The company's 1979 profits amounted to 54m UAE Dirhams (34m Dirhams in 1978). On capital amounting to US$ 200m, the profits continued to soar; in 1981 net profit came to US$ 59,865,656,[50] based on the company's prestige, the persistent strength of its shares, and the diversity of its investment.

In spite of the Sharjah Group's major regional and international role and its good reputation, it overreached itself in establishing too many companies, and in engaging too heavily in share trading and speculation for the sake of rapid and large profits. After the crash in 1982, the company was no longer able to achieve its goals; its net profit decreased to US$ 11m in 1982 (US$ 60m in 1981). In 1983, the company's losses amounted to US$ 15,255,844m,[51] caused by the crisis of Souq al-Manakh.

Gulf Investment and Real Estate Company, the other big investment institution in the area, invested heavily in property, traded on the stock exchange and took equity in other companies. It built residential complexes, acquired a hotel in Sharjah, real estate in Bahrain and came in on property deals in Egypt and France. In France, the company acquired a stake of US$ 7.5m in the Nice Real Estate Company, whose capital base was US$ 22m. In Egypt, the company acquired a stake in International Towers of Egypt. Its presence in the stock market pushed net profits from 54m Dirhams in 1979 to 167m Dirhams in 1981. The company also had shares in multinational companies, and in banks in Hong Kong and the United States. At regional level, it had shares in the Arab Sahil Bank of Ras Al-Khaimah, the First Gulf Bank of Ajman and the Gulf United Bank of Bahrain.

In the aftermath of the crash, the company managed to stand its ground in view of its strong financial position and because it had not involved itself deeply in the stock market. However, its activity was subdued, and will probably not recover before the recovery of the stock market. Net profit decreased in 1982 to 4,739,813 Dirhams after the Manakh crisis. The company earmarked 345m Dirhams to cover probable losses arising from bad debts, because dealers were unable to meet their obligations fully. As so large a bad debt provision was unforeseen, it was bound to affect net profit adversely.[52]

The Arab Company for General Investments, popularly known as *Shua'a,* is the region's third big investment group. Founded in 1979, its shareholders ranged from individuals and Arab Chambers of Commerce, to the Government of Dubai, whose share amounted to 27 per cent. It was the only Gulf company to procure a licence from the Emirate of Dubai. Pushing strongly into the arena of investment, finance and new projects, Shua'a enjoyed a powerful financial structure derived from its heavyweight founders and support from Arab States.[53]

Pearl Investment was founded in 1979. Licensed in Bahrain, it undertook local, regional and foreign investment. It founded the Kuwait Bank in

Paris and took a 25 per cent stake in the equity of Dubai nationals. It bought into Bank of America and other enterprises in addition to its share trading and establishing new companies.[54]

Kuwait and Gulf Financial Centre Company, incorporated in Ajman in 1979, had few interests other than holdings in other companies, and speculation in shares.

Gulf Financial Centre Company, incorporated in Sharjah (Emiri Decree No. 57/1979) with fully paid-up capital of 200m UAE Dirhams, held 8.75 per cent of the National Bank of Sharjah; 36.72 per cent of Sharjah Insurance Company, and about 11.36 per cent of the London-based Arab International Company. It also had a stake in the Bahrain and Middle East Bank, the Arab Investment Bank, the International Hotels Company and the Drugs Company, and was active in foreign exchange markets. Net profits in 1980 amounted to 95m Dirhams, equivalent to 47.5 per cent of paid-up capital. In its second year, profits jumped to 174.14m Dirhams, equivalent to 78.25 per cent of paid-up capital. This attested to the company's success and its ability to create large profits.

The board's mistake was to fragment the shares seven times and convert the capital from UAE Dirhams to US Dollars: authorised capital became US$ 220m and paid-up capital US$ 110m. The company had overextended its shareholdings in other Gulf companies; and it had acquired a vast portfolio. The company was unable to stand its ground when the stock market collapsed, and net profit in 1982 amounted to US$ 8,527,500.[55] A major part of the company's capital was lost.

Other investment companies followed the same path as the ones already examined, but did not manage to reach their size. Some, such as the Bahrain and Kuwait Investment Group (formerly the Dubai Group), managed to stay intact with a diversity of investments.

Generally speaking, no Gulf investment company, whether industrious and profitable or one of those which did not do well, can be said to have made any positive achievements, if judged from the point of view of the national economy of the licensing states. They contributed almost nothing by way of long-term economic development schemes whether at national or regional level, or ambitious projects which could have helped to promote badly needed technical skills. At the outset, all these companies publicised their serious economic intentions towards investment in the service of the national economy. It was soon apparent that their enthusiasm was devoted purely to quick personal gain by the systematic manipulation of the stock exchange. The banking sector had a relatively more useful impact, but this could be controversial. For instance, the First Gulf Bank and the Arab Sahil Bank, the only two public company Gulf banks in the UAE, did not contribute substantially to the UAE economy in terms of economic development, though this could be because they were established relatively late. The founders of both banks, and particularly the Kuwaitis among them, were able to use them as an effective financial medium and shop window. First Gulf Bank especially was active during the years 1980 and 1981, deriving handsome profits from deposits and share subscriptions for the non-stop stream of new companies. The UAE Central Bank notified the two banks that, to qualify for the category of 'national bank', they had to adjust their capital equity so that 80 per cent was allotted to UAE nationals. Nothing has happened at the time of writing, and therefore the existing equity structure remains: 51 per cent for UAE nationals and 49 per cent for Kuwaitis in First Gulf Bank; 60 per cent,[56] for UAE nationals in the Arab Sahil Bank. Since bank accountability in the UAE has been unified under the Central Bank, First Gulf and Arab Sahil Bank may begin to play a more serious role in the national economy. Better still, they may be transformed into National Banks.

Kuwaiti investors were also quick to benefit from the system of offshore banking units introduced in Bahrain and used by numerous Arab and foreign banking institutions. Four public Gulf banks, United Gulf, Bahrain International, Bahrain and Middle East, and Arabian Investment, were accordingly opened in Bahrain. The latter was directed by a number of prominent financiers, and undertook foreign investment activities.[57]

Established relatively late, from the surpluses accumulated by companies and individuals during the market boom years, these banks did not involve themselves deeply in the Kuwait Stock Market, and managed to stay financially intact.

Being in Bahrain, these banks contributed, though modestly, to the national economy. They provided employment and training for numerous young people, and helped in development projects.[58]

Insurance Companies

The insurance sector amongst Gulf companies is represented by five companies: Gulf Union Insurance and the Arab International Insurance Company in Bahrain; United Insurance Company in Ras Al-Khaimah (founded in 1976, it is one of the earliest Gulf public companies); Sharjah Insurance and Re-insurance Company in Sharjah; and International

Insurance Company in Ajman.[59]

These companies contributed nothing to the licence-granting states in terms of economic development, whether at local or regional level. The companies' original objectives had, anyway, little to do with the needs of economic development in the region. Their chief purpose was enrolment on the stock exchange in order to profit from trading their shares.

As far as the insurance sector was concerned, the introduction of these companies was superfluous because of the presence of sufficient already established local insurance companies. These newly-introduced companies are now suffering from lack of adequate business and the large losses resulting from their involvement in the stock market after its collapse.

Industrial and Production Companies

This sector could be the best of the activity-sectors amongst Gulf companies. It has made a remarkable contribution to the economy of the UAE as an instrument for raising income, diversifying resources and broadening the base of production. Some have played an important part in the local, as well as the regional economy, particularly those operating in the fields of cement production, agricultural development, pharmaceuticals and medical equipment, poultry and dairy farms.

Although not all these companies went into production, they did serve their countries of domicile. The majority of investment companies (see above), however, were positively beneficial only to the countries in which they operated, rather than the countries of domicile in which they kept only token offices run by minor employees.

The industrial and production sector of Gulf public companies consisted of about 24[60] — 20 in the UAE and 4 in Bahrain. Six specialised in cement production. Up to mid-1984, their total output (actual and estimated) amounted to about 4,020,000 tons distributed as follows:[61]

Gulf cement	1,000,000 tons (to be raised to 2.5m tons)
Sharjah cement	1,300,000 tons
Fujairah cement	520,000 tons
Ajman cement	500,000 tons (started production on 1st April 1984)
White cement	200,000 tons
Umm Al-Qaiwain cement	500,000 tons (production not yet begun)
Total	4,020,000 tons

The plants of the nationally owned companies in the UAE, and Al-Ain and Ras Al-Khaimah in Dubai, managed, to a great extent, to meet local and regional needs, and contributed to the national income in their country of domicile. This is reflected in their investment in production assets, and in their employment of technical and professional skills, as well as in their marketing and exports.

Perhaps the only negative aspect of these companies was their lack of coordination in production and planning, although this can be put down to the lack of regulation exerted by the UAE Ministry of Industry on the organisation of local industry, particularly at federal level. This left the Emirates to act independently of one another.

Chaos was inevitable. The plants, blindly responding to short-term demand, failed to take into consideration long-term market conditions. Consequently, and also as a result of the emergence of similar plants in other Gulf States, the local market became saturated. The situation was further aggravated by sharp cuts in demand, after the completion of several infrastructure projects and the peaking of the construction boom. The 1983 budgets of most of these companies reflect direct losses. For example, Sharjah Cement and the Industrial Development Company made net profits of 18m Dirhams in 1978, 29m Dirhams in 1980, and 71m in 1981 — profits made, in 1980–81, not from the main business of the company, cement sales, but from speculation. In 1982, when most companies either ended with lower profits or straight losses, Sharjah Cement's profits fell to 55m Dirhams (Table 2.3). In 1983, the company had losses of 48,510,831m Dirhams, brought on by the Manakh crash and the collapse of share prices.[62]

The same fate confronted most Gulf companies addicted to speculation in Souq Al-Manakh. In addition the UAE, with its small population, was over-producing cement. If the construction boom had not subsided and the stock market collapsed, the country would have continued establishing more cement plants. Nevertheless, the owners of these cement plants are optimistic: they pin their hopes on a revival of the market either as a result of improvement in the international oil market, or with the end of hostilities in the Iraq-Iran war, and the reconstruction projects in the aftermath of the war. A further reason for optimism is that, through the Gulf Cooperation Council, the Gulf States may begin to support their local industries.[63]

Up to the time of writing four Gulf companies are operating in the agricultural and animal production sectors but only one, Gulf Agriculture Development Company, has realised some of its genuine objectives. It established a poultry farm in Sharjah, producing eggs

(30 million in 1982) and birds for the market. It also built a fodder processing plant and a number of granaries at Khalid, the port of Sharjah. It also managed the International Nursery Farm Company and the Ra'ad Foodstuffs Company in Kuwait. This company, too, suffered as a result of the market collapse. Its accounts for the year 1982 show a loss of 2,075,968 Dirhams, compared to a profit of 127,689,367 Dirhams in 1981, and 18,201,321 Dirhams in 1980. The reason for most of these profits was probably because of substantial gains made from the sales of shares, securities and property, which amounted to 122m Dirhams in 1981. In other words, its major sources of profit were through trading shares not production.[64] (Table 2.3.)

Ras Al-Khaimah Poultry and Fodder did at least establish one small fodder processing plant and the Chicken Production Farm.[65] Gulf Livestock, and Gulf Animal Resources, both founded in 1982, the year of the collapse of the stock market, inevitably failed and may have lost part of their capital in share-trading immediately upon opening for business.

Gulf Industrial was the one company operating in the chrome industry. In 1981, it also established a factory for the manufacture of household stainless steel appliances and metal office equipment, whose output amounted to 60 thousand units. The company has its own sales showroom in both the UAE and Kuwait but its achievements did not go beyond this.[66]

Mining and Industry Company, which was founded in Ajman in 1979, was supposed to operate in the sphere of cement, mining and quarries, but undertook no noticeable activity in that direction.

Arab Iron and Steel carried out projects in Bahrain, the most important of which was an iron refining plant. However, the proprietors admitted that their plant would be in difficulties for years to come because of foreign competition and high transport costs.

The Petroleum Products Company undertook, in collaboration with foreign firms, oil prospecting and well-digging operations in Ajman. Prospects look good.

The United Gulf Industry and Services Company carried out work in the contracting sector, especially in Saudi Arabia, and was involved in maintenance. It also took part in the Ajman oil prospecting operations.

The Emirates Kalankar Company, incorporated in Fujairah, had not (to the time of writing) started any business. When demand for cement products began to shrink, the company's cement project was frozen. The company may be liquidated and its assets merged with Fujairah Cement.

Pharmaceutical and medical instrument companies have fared better than most, and done what they set out to do. For example, Gulf Drug Industries went into production in 1984, with signed export contracts to countries of the Gulf Cooperation Council (GCC). Gulf Medical Projects opened the up-to-date private Sharjah Zahra Hospital, with a Chinese acupuncture clinic attached. The company had also taken a stake in a plant in Kuwait that manufactures disposable syringes, and has invested in a modern children's hospital in London.[67]

In the hotels' sector, International Hotels has done nothing substantial on home ground in the several years since it was founded, though it has invested in hotel enterprises in North Yemen and Egypt.[68]

The object of this brief review of the achievements of the Gulf companies in their countries of domicile was to examine to what extent these companies had realised the objectives they originally proclaimed in the service of the national economy through the diversification of resources and the promotion of technical skills. It is clear that the founding directors were primarily preoccupied with quick profit-taking from high speed speculations in shares. This inevitably made them oblivious to the real objectives of their companies and their economic viability.

Table 2.3 shows the profit and loss of Gulf companies in relation to capital. Representative companies were selected from the investment sector, property, industry, banking and insurance. The table reflects the high profit percentages realised during the years 1979–80–81 which were the boom years for the Al-Manakh stock market. Examination of the company budgets suggests that the greater share of profits was attributed to share trading, rather than real business. The decrease in profits or the losses incurred in 1982–83 were direct results of the suspension of share trading after the collapse of Al-Manakh at the end of 1982. Companies deeply involved in deferred payment transactions were hit especially hard because individual and institutional bankruptcies meant they could no longer redeem their entitlements.

The evidence is that the goal of these companies was to trade their shares in the stock market and not to achieve either benefit, development or productivity for the economies of the licence-granting States.

Economic Impact and Results

As Gulf companies became a reality in the lives of the people of the Gulf States, businessmen and even small traders became more sophisticated in shares and securities trading, and investors in the Gulf States, particularly the UAE and Bahrain, were attracted by the prospect

Table 2.3: Gulf Company Profit and Loss Figures 1979–83

Company	Year	Capital (million)	Net profit (million)	Loss (million)	Percentage
Gulf Investment and Real Estate	1979	Dh 75	Dh 54		72%
	1980	Dh 175	Dh 45		26%
	1981	Dh 293	Dh 167		56%
	1982	Dh 592	Dh 5		0.84%
	1983	Dh 592		Dh 284	(48%)
Sharjah Cement and Industrial Development	1979	Dh 150	Dh 18		12%
	1980	Dh 180	Dh 29		16%
	1981	Dh 275	Dh 71		26%
	1982	Dh 481	Dh 55		11%
	1983	Dh 505		Dh 48	10%
Gulf Medical Projects (incorporated in 1979)	1979	—	—	—	—
	1980	Dh 102	Dh 54		53%
	1981	Dh 123	Dh 55		45%
	1982	Dh 235		Dh 39	(17%)
	1983	Dh 235		Dh 47	(20%)
Gulf Agriculture and Development	1979	Dh 50	Dh 11		22%
	1980	Dh 99	Dh 18		18%
	1981	Dh 115	Dh 128		111%
	1982	Dh 200		Dh 2	1%
	1983[1]				
Sharjah Group	1979	Dh 250	Dh 54		22%
	1980[2]	US$ 82	US$ 20		24%
	1981	US$ 130	US$ 60		46%
	1982	US$ 199	US$ 11		6%
	1983	US$ 200		US$ 15	(63%)
Gulf Financial Centre (incorporated in 1979)	1979	—	—	—	—
	1980	Dh 200	Dh 95		48%
	1981[3]	US$ 60	US$ 47		78%
	1982	US$ 110	US$ 8		7%
	1983	US$ 110		US$ 14	(13%)
First Gulf Bank	1979	Dh 114	Dh 10		9%
	1980	Dh 119	Dh 30		25%
	1981	Dh 119	Dh 34		29%
	1982	Dh 119	Dh 26		22%
	1983	Dh 119	Dh 17		14%
Sharjah Insurance and Re-insurance	1979	Dh 6,900	Dh 3		0.42%
	1980	Dh 49	Dh 9		18%
	1981	Dh 50	Dh 32		64%
	1982	Dh 100		Dh 4	(4%)
	1983	Dh 100		Dh 16	(16%)

1. 1983 budget was unpublished because the company's activity slumped after incurring heavy losses.
2. In 1980 capital was converted from Dirhams to US Dollars.
3. In 1981 capital was converted from Dirhams to US Dollars.
Source: Company Financial Statements and Annual Reports for the years 1979–83

✓

of founding companies with Kuwaiti partners.

The licence-granting authorities and their countries reaped considerable financial rewards as the number of new companies grew, by having a large stake in most of them, particularly during the boom years 1979–81. Most of these nationals, especially those with limited incomes, would sell their shares for a profit of 50 per cent of the share value. In another development, those without the resources to buy shares used to trade their nationality certificates or passports to non-nationals for 150 to 300 UAE Dirhams, or 15 to 30 Bahraini Dinars, who would subscribe on their behalf at an agreed price. This was a device used by foreign investors to get round conditions governing the acquisition of shares offered to the public. One condition obliged share buyers to produce a certificate of nationality or passport to prove that they were nationals of the licence-granting state before they were permitted to buy. This phenomenon of trading nationality documents developed in Kuwait during the sixties alongside the phenomenon of establishing Kuwaiti companies. People packing the offices of share dealers and stock brokers so as to hand over their identity cards for a modest sum in cash during the registration period became a common sight. Before the practice was prohibited, people would trade the card to more than one buyer by reproducing photocopies.[69]

At first, the formation of Gulf companies allowed banks in Kuwait, the UAE and Bahrain to flourish. Their balance sheets indicate that the banks which used to deal with these companies, taking deposits or giving loans to invest in shares, realised handsome profits.[70] Banks in Kuwait reaped substantial benefits from loans granted to company founders or prospective shareholders during the early days in the life of a new company. Banks in the UAE also did well in the years 1979, 1980 and 1981, when net profits represented 25 per cent of capital. However, this proportion shrank to 18 per cent, then to 15 per cent[71] after the collapse of the stock market and the prohibition on establishing new companies. The period also witnessed an abnormal surge in transactions between financial institutions in the UAE, Bahrain and Kuwait. The constant movement of capital from the licence-granting countries to Kuwait, and the transfer of the values of shares sold in the Al-Manakh stock market in Kuwait to other Gulf countries shifted billions of UAE Dirhams from the Kuwait market to the UAE during the years 1979 to 1982.

The typical UAE investor, though street-wise as an investor was not yet a speculator and settled for quick and limited profit-taking from share selling to Kuwaiti investors.

The massive wealth accumulated by some Kuwaitis from the performance of their Gulf companies and speculations in Al-Manakh stock market, prompted them to search for places to invest. The result was a crop of Gulf holding companies that controlled international firms and banks in many countries in the world. Financial and industrial institutions, wholly or partly owned by Kuwaiti investors, sprang up in the United States, Britain, and France as well as parts of the Arab world and the Far East. The institutions stand as examples of useful multinational ventures.[72]

The artificial inflation in share prices forced the UAE Central Bank to issue a warning and to take preliminary steps towards establishing a disciplined stock exchange in the UAE. A committee was set up comprising members of government departments and chambers of commerce and specialists, but unforeseen factors, including the collapse of the stock market in Kuwait in August 1982, economic deterioration resulting from the continuing Iraq-Iran armed conflict and the Lebanese civil war as well as the fall in oil prices and production prevented these discussions from going any further at the time. In another development, licence-granting Emirates, led strongly by the Emirate of Sharjah, stopped issuing licences for Gulf companies and imposed controls over the activities of existing ones. Government officials met board members to learn at first hand how the companies were run.

The Emirate of Sharjah issued the first law of its type in the UAE, the Dealers and Stockbrokers Ordinance No. 1/1981,[73] at a time when offices opened by often inexperienced dealers and stockbrokers were springing up everywhere and subject to no well-defined legal restrictions. Section 6 of the Ordinance provides that the dealers who handle cash transactions involving buyer and seller, should be required to exercise professional integrity. A dealer had to be:

A national of the UAE.
At least 18 years of age and have sufficient experience in commercial business.
A person of reputable conduct who has not sustained bankruptcy or been convicted of a criminal offence.
Of financial standing, and able to present to the authorities any financial or property guarantees required of him.

The Ordinance also specified dealers' fees and obligations, as well as appropriate punishments.

The measures reflected the anxiety of the authorities in the licence-granting Emirates and States that the continuing chaos created by the

Gulf companies would ultimately lead to catastrophe.

The emergence and continuing presence of Gulf companies highlighted the lack of adequate company laws and regulations in some regions, and the multiplicity of licence-granting authorities.

In the UAE particularly, the absence of binding policies and long-term plans in the spheres of industry, commerce and investment, at Federal level, confined the Federal Ministries of Commerce and Economics and Planning to issuing regulations they could not enforce. At the same time, individual Emirates continued to exercise their freedom to issue locally binding decrees, without obligation to refer to the federal authorities. The Gulf companies spared no effort to exploit these opportunities. As a result, the local market was soon to be saturated with cement plants, poultry farms, and investment and insurance companies. Even in Bahrain, where licence-granting is vested in a single government authority and where company laws exist, the greater attraction of highly-profitable investment during the boom years meant that the flood of licences continued in the sectors of banking, insurance, investment and industry. Despite the damage created by all these overlapping projects, Bahrain did benefit from the employment opportunities. The fact that a great number of young, educated Bahrainis found jobs and training in the new companies is in itself a positive achievement.

The Kuwaiti Ministry of Commerce and Industry, concerned by the negative impact of the Gulf companies on the Kuwaiti stock exchange and the share prices of Kuwaiti companies, issued licences to establish Kuwaiti closed and limited-liability companies.[74] Kuwaiti investors rushed to form such companies, whose shares were soon traded in the Al-Manakh stock market alongside those of Gulf public companies. The closed Kuwaiti companies became one of the major factors leading to the deterioration and ultimate collapse of the stock market.

An important outcome of the phenomenon of the Gulf holding companies was the emergence in Kuwait of a special stock market for these companies, which sprang up after 'Gulf' shares were banned on the Kuwaiti stock exchange. Known formally as the 'parallel' or 'minor' stock exchange, it is better known among the share-trading public as Al-Manakh. The speed with which this stock market grew and flourished was startling, so that it soon became one of the largest in the world in terms of volume of trading, market value of shares, and the volume of post-dated cheque transactions.

The collective structure of the capital of Gulf companies and their multi-purpose nature makes them joint enterprises worthy of serious study, despite their devotion to share trading and speculation. Had their joint nature been properly exploited, they would have provided the best vehicles for constructive economic cooperation at regional level. Of all the regional groupings in the world, the Gulf States most need to cooperate to create the broad industrial base that should provide additional sources of income to oil. With a small population, but also oil-rich, the Gulf States need to pool their resources so as to exploit the economic benefits of their skills, capital assets and markets on a large scale. Such cooperation could have helped to create a large economic group with considerable impact, regionally and internationally. This is exactly what the founders of Gulf public companies failed to perceive. Instead of becoming instruments of economic development, these institutions were financially wasteful and squandered genuine economic potential in ideal circumstances.

Notes

1. Al-Manakh in Arabic literally means the resting place for camels. (In persuading his camel to rest, a camel owner repeats loudly the word 'Nakh'.)
2. Rīād al-Abrash, 'Phenomenon of Gulf shareholding companies', a paper submitted to the Conference on the Development of the Stock Market in Kuwait between 14th and 16th November 1981, (Kuwait: Kuwaiti Chamber of Commerce and Industry, 1981), p. 366.
3. See Chapter 1, p. 13–14.
4. Salem Marzouq Al Tuhaih, *The Securities Market in Kuwait*, (Kuwait: The Emiri Diwan, Office of Research to his Highness the Amir, 1983), p. 8.
5. Fāyz Kartūtlī, supplement on Gulf public companies, *Al Seyassah* [Kuwait: newspaper] No. 4927, 17.3.82, p. 52.
6. For Law No. 15/1960, see Chapter 1, p. 7–8.
7. 'The Story of the Illegitimate Child who Surpassed the Legitimate Sons', *Al Watan* [Kuwait: newspaper], 3.11.84, p. 10.
8. Study prepared by the Department of Economic Studies and Research, *Offshore Banking Units and Exempted Companies in Bahrain, 1975–82*, (Bahrain: Bahraini Chamber of Commerce and Industry, 1982), p. 13.
9. Federal Law No. 8/1984, concerning trading companies in UAE, *Official Gazette*, No. 137, April 1984.
10. See for example, the Sharjah Group and the Gulf Financial Centre: Memorandum of Association and Articles of Associations (MA and AA) and list of founders.
11. Sharjah Group MA and AA, Emiri Decree No. 133/76, issued 16.11.76.
12. Sharjah Group, list of founders.
13. See the Gulf Financial Centre and Sharjah Cement and Industrial Development, MA and AA, and list of founders.
14. Sharjah Group, MA and AA.
15. *Fifth Annual Report* of the Sharjah Group, 1980–81.
16. United Insurance, MA and AA, Emiri Decree No. 24/1977.
17. 'Collapse of the Al-Manakh Empire', *Al-Khaleej*, [Sharjah: newspaper] No. 1261, 21.9.82, p. 6.
18. Gulf Agriculture Development, MA and AA, Emiri Decree No. 105/1977, 2.6.77.

19. *Annual Reports*: Gulf Agriculture Development, 1977–82.
20. See board of directors' list in the MA and AA of Gulf Agriculture Development 1977.
21. Gulf Investment and Real Estate, MA and AA, Emiri Decree No. 2 issued 12.1.77.
22. *Annual Reports*: Gulf Investment and Real Estate 1977–82.
23. Ibid.
24. Gulf Industries Co, MA and AA, Emiri Decree No. 133/1977, issued 29.6.77.
25. Section 3 of Decree No. 133/1977, Gulf Industries.
26. Gulf Cement, MA and AA, Emiri Decree No. 24/1977.
27. Ibid, and list of founders.
28. Capital adjusted in Emiri Decree No. 10/1981, for Gulf Cement.
29. Al-Abrash, 'Phenomenon of Gulf Public Companies', p. 373.
30. 'The Kuwait Stock Exchange — from chaos to controlled dealing', *Al Watan*, 29.9.84, p. 11.
31. See Act Decree No. 3/1975.
32. Article 5, Articles of Association, Gulf Medical Projects, Emiri Decree No. 48/1979.
33. Article 11, Articles of Association, Gulf Investments, 1977.
34. Article 7, Articles of Association, Kuwait and Gulf Financial, 1979; see too, Al-Abrash, 'Phenomenon of Gulf Public Companies', p. 377.
35. Lists of founders of Gulf companies.
36. Al-Abrash, 'Phenomenon of Gulf Public Companies', p. 376.
37. As for instance the Accounts Office of Ernest & Whinney; and the Office of Bader Al-Bazie & Co, which are in Kuwait.
38. 'Mysteries of Speculation in Kuwait', *Al Bayan*, No. 628, 4.2.82, p. 3.
39. *Annual Reports* of, for example, Gulf Financial Centre Co in Sharjah, and Gulf Agriculture Co in Sharjah.
40. *Al-Khaleej*, No. 1261, 21.9.82, p. 6.
41. *Al-Khaleej*, 24.6.84, pp. 1 and 5.
42. *Al-Khaleej*, 18.12.84, p. 1.
43. For example, Yūsuf Al-Muzaynī's name appears simultaneously on the board of Gulf Financial Centre of Sharjah, Sharjah Insurance, Umm Al-Qaiwain Gas, Emirates Kalankar, and Bank of Bahrain and Middle East.
44. List of founders, MA and AA.
45. *Annual Reports* of, for example, the Sharjah Group.
46. *Annual Reports*: Gulf Financial Centre of Sharjah, 1981–82.
47. Al-Fujairah Kalankar, put issue allowances up to 10 per cent.
48. See Table 2.1.
49. *Annual Reports* of the Sharjah Group, 1978–79.
50. When the company converted the capital from UAE Dirhams to US$ in 1980, see the company's *Annual Report*: 1980–81.
51. The Profit and Loss Statement, 30.12.83, Sharjah Group, published in *Al-Khaleej*, No. 1849, 5.5.84.
52. *Annual Reports*: Gulf Investment and Real Estate, 1979–82. See also Table 2.3.
53. Arab Company for General Investments, MA and AA, 1979.
54. *Annual Reports*: Pearl Investment Company, 1979–82.
55. *Annual Reports and Financial Statements*: Gulf Financial Centre, 1980–82.
56. *Annual Reports*: First Gulf Bank, and the Arab Sāhil Bank, 1980–82.
57. *Offshore Banking Units and Exempted Companies, 1979–82*, p. 25.
58. *Offshore Banking*, p. 17.
59. See Table 2.1.
60. See Table 2.1.
61. *Annual Reports*: Sharjah Cement, Fujairah Cement, Ajman Cement, White Cement, Umm Al-Qaiwain Cement, 1983–84.
62. *Annual Reports and Financial Statements*: Sharjah Cement and Industrial

Development, 1979–83.

63. *Al-Khaleej*, No. 2030, 10.11.84, p. 4.

64. *Annual Reports and Financial Statements*: Gulf Agriculture Development, 1979–82.

65. *Annual Reports*: Ras Al-Khaimah Poultry and Fodder, 1981–82.

66. *Annual Reports*: Gulf Industries, 1981–82.

67. *Annual Report*: Gulf Drug Industries, 1981; and *Annual Reports*: Gulf Medical Projects, 1980–82.

68. *Annual Reports*: International Hotels, 1980–82.

69. Verbal information obtained from brokers' offices in the Emirates of Sharjah, (Arab commercial centre, and Gulf economic company), 12.6.84.

70. *Annual Reports*: First Gulf Bank, 1981–83; Sharjah National Bank, Investment Bank in Sharjah 1980–83.

71. Ibid.

72. *Financial Statement*: Arabian Investment Banking Corporation: Bahrain 1983; also, 'Arab Bank buys in Los Angeles', *Financial Times*, 3.2.84; also see *Annual Reports*: Coast Investment Development, PSC, Ras Al-Khaimah 1982–83; see also Chapter 2, p. 38–46, Achievements of Gulf Companies.

73. Dealers and Stockbrokers Ordinance Law No. 1/1981, issued by the Ruler of Sharjah on 1.5.81.

74. al-Tuhaih, S.M., *The Securities Market*, p. 15.

3

Gulf Stock Exchange

Emergence and Development of the Gulf Stock Exchange in Kuwait

The emergence of a Gulf stock exchange was only logical in view of the fact that the Gulf companies were prohibited from trading their shares on the official Kuwaiti stock exchange. The volume of trading on the Gulf stock exchange soon surpassed that of the Kuwait exchange. As the Gulf stock exchange passed through three phases of development, the study is divided as follows: first stage, 1976–78; second stage, 1978–82; third stage, 1982–84.

First Stage: 1976–78

The emergence of the Gulf stock exchange in Kuwait coincided with the birth of the first Gulf public company. The site was a market where shares of Kuwaiti incorporated companies were once traded, known as Souq Al-Jat — the Jat Market (*Jat* means clover, in Arabic, a widely-used fodder). The market was in the midst of the congested commercial area. The women traders would sit behind their displays of milk products, Arab medicines, women's garments, and clover and local goods of every kind. The market also housed a number of small shops which specialised in clothes, Arab perfumes and locally made shoes. Scattered amongst the shops were offices of brokers of property and stocks. These offices and pavements constituted the nucleus of the Kuwaiti stock exchange. As more and more companies were established and investment awareness grew, trading in shares began to flourish.

It was natural that it was in this market that the shares of the first Gulf company were offered for trading. The brokers welcomed the newcomer with spontaneous enthusiasm, regarding it as a sign of wider activity in the stock market. The first Gulf company offered its shares allotted for general subscription in November 1976[1] in Kuwait. Subscribers responded in large numbers. The banks appointed for the dealings were crowded with brokers publicising the new institution. Despite the enthusiastic welcome, irregularities occurred. Gamblers illegally traded shares before they had been sorted and allotted and before subscribers knew the number allotted to them. Share prices increased to KD 4 on a face value of 300 fils.

The illegal practice gave the Kuwaiti Ministry of Commerce and Industry a pretext to intervene, and the offering of the company's shares for general subscription in Kuwait was banned by the ministerial resolution issued on 6th December 1976,[2] on the grounds that this was not a one hundred per cent Kuwaiti company, unlicensed by the Kuwaiti Ministry, according to law No. 3/1975. It was the first official Kuwaiti intervention to confront Gulf companies and the Gulf stock exchange. The subscription process was transferred to the licensing authority of the Emirate of Sharjah. However, the ordinary trading of the company's shares in the Jat Market continued uninterrupted. In 1977, Kuwaiti incorporated companies moved to the new stock exchange inaugurated that year; officially-recognised brokers who remained in Souq Al-Jat continued dealing in shares of the unlawful Gulf companies and in those of Kuwaiti incorporated share companies which fell short of conditions decreed by the new stock exchange. The striking success of the first Gulf company encouraged Kuwaiti investors to consider founding similar companies in the UAE. Four sprang up in 1977, two in Sharjah, and one in Ras Al-Khaimah and in Ajman. This had the effect of bringing the Kuwaiti investor nearer to the long-cherished goal of establishing Gulf companies in the Gulf States, using Kuwait itself as the market in which to trade the shares of the new companies. The development opened the doors to the creation of a stock market, similar to the Kuwaiti one, in other Gulf States, so as to enlarge the scope of share-trading.

It is hard to obtain reliable data and statistics about daily volumes of trading or average market prices during this early stage of the Gulf stock market, because no regulations obliged brokers to keep systematic records. The custom was for the broker to conduct a share deal between seller and buyer, and record the particulars, including his commission, on a slip of paper. Once the names of seller and buyer had been recorded for the purposes of the transfer of the card, the accumulated slips were thrown out, as there was no good reason to keep them. Brokers who ran their business from the roadside were equipped with no more than a briefcase stuffed with share certificates. These brokers would write down the necessary facts, if they were literate, or would ask a colleague to do it in a small notebook, so as to be able to refer back.[3]

As the Gulf stock exchange showed no signs of disappearing, owners of Gulf companies and large investors took steps to have its presence regularised, because the Kuwaiti 1960 and 1975 laws could not be applied to Gulf companies and, in fact, made them unlawful. The Kuwaiti Ministry of Commerce and Industry remained silent. Investors and brokers concluded — correctly — that this indicated official consent, escalated their business activities in the market and created more and more companies. The kings of the market went about convincing others that the government would never close the market, for the following reasons:

> Gulf companies held large sums of Kuwaiti money, in capital and interest; any action against them would seriously undermine a section of Kuwaiti nationals.
>
> Kuwait's inclination was to safeguard the tradition of *laissez faire* as the basis of the Kuwaiti economic system, as long as it did not conflict with national interest and economic development.
>
> The growing strength of the economic and social forces behind Gulf companies and their influence on share prices.[4]

The Kuwaiti Goverment continued tacitly to permit the shares of these companies to be traded. Away from the official stock exchange, dealers and propagators of Gulf shares continued, untroubled, playing their commercial game in Souq Al-Jat. Large profits began to pour in, with dealers getting commissions of half a Kuwaiti fil for every share sold. Share bears also took profits, as high as 300 per cent of the face value of the shares. The absence of laws and regulations allowed the dealers unrestricted freedom in deciding the price of shares. For investors, it was difficult, if not impossible, to make a meaningful appraisal of prices. Reliable information about general trends in the market and authentic data about each company did not exist.

Quantities traded grew steadily in 1976 at rapidly rising prices. This followed a temporary recession in the Kuwait stock exchange in 1974 when prices and the volume of trading shrank, only to revive in earnest in 1975–76. The birth of the Gulf stock exchange in 1976, coinciding with this revival, reflected the growing demand for shares. The birth of the Gulf stock exchange and the establishment of the first Gulf companies could not have come at a better time and pioneer Gulf companies rapidly went into profit.

A multiplicity of factors, connected directly or indirectly with the oil boom, helped to make 1976 a year of abnormal prosperity.[5]

1. The sudden escalation in oil prices in 1974–75, resulting in a flow of oil revenues at growing rates, triggered off a period of unprecedented economic prosperity in all sectors. The government in Kuwait undertook vast development and investment programmes. Because the boom led to rapid increases in the price of land and buildings and large profits for property companies, speculation in land and property was reflected in the stock market.

2. Liquidity grew by 24 per cent in 1975 and 37 per cent in 1976, under the impetus of growing government expenditure, and the flood of capital withdrawn from abroad by big Kuwaiti investors when world rates of interest fell. The local capital market was overflowing with money, at a time when only the stock market and the property sector were ready to absorb it.

Thus the year 1976 heralded a golden age for both the Kuwaiti and the Gulf stock exchanges. The volume of trading at Souq Al-Jat amounted to 19.8 million share transactions in 1976, which included shares of locally incorporated Kuwaiti companies using this stock market, as well as the Sharjah Group.

The boom stampeded investors into blind speculation. Consequently, and without apparent reason, the stock market began to slow down in early 1977: trading volume slumped by 31 per cent compared to 1976, to 13.7 million transactions, and the face value of shares registered a marked decrease.[6] The government had to intervene to safeguard and stabilise both the official market and, indirectly, the non-official Gulf stock exchange. The official measures may have been a factor in activating the non-official stock exchange, easing the way for still more Gulf companies. One measure to stabilise the market was a Ministerial decree issued to organise deferred-payment transactions under the supervision of the Ministry of Commerce. In August 1977, two other decrees were issued: one banned the establishment of more Kuwaiti public companies, the other prohibited increases in company capital except within narrow limits.[7] These and other measures applied only to locally incorporated Kuwaiti companies and the Kuwaiti Stock Exchange. Gulf companies and Souq Al-Jat, as well as unqualified local Kuwaiti companies, were outside the jurisdiction of Kuwaiti law and applied only those measures that suited them.

Nevertheless, the impact of government intervention helped the market to shake off the effects of the recession in 1978. Owners of Gulf companies founded in 1977 saw in the post-recession period an opportunity to make profits. Two years of share trading of Gulf holding companies in Kuwait were enough to convince investors and company founders that the Gulf stock exchange had become a reality and was there to stay. During this period, Gulf shares were acquired and traded by almost every investor, particularly in 1978 when small savers entered the arena in large numbers. It was time to enlarge and consolidate this stock exchange, and investors felt sure it had outlived all threats to close it. That was how the Gulf stock exchange came of age, and developed unhindered.

Second Stage: 1978–82 — Emergence of Souq Al-Manakh

Once the Gulf stock exchange had established itself as a dynamic reality in the Kuwaiti commercial arena, the kings and brokers of the market realised that the wretched stalls and scattered offices at the disorganised Souq Al-Jat no longer suited the fast growing trade in Gulf shares. Indeed, Souq Al-Jat was neither designed nor fit for share-trading; its geographical remoteness from the heart of commercial and financial life in the city was another disadvantage.

Thus, in May 1978 a two-storey complex, owned by the Kuwaiti International Investment Company, was rented. The first floor was divided into offices and the landlord, the Kuwaiti International Investment Company, made it a condition that these offices should be rented only to share brokers and property dealers. There was car parking in the basement. The building was known as Al-Manakh, after the area. Once the dealers moved in, it became Souq Al-Manakh, or Al-Manakh Market. In formal documents, it came to be known as the parallel market — parallel to the Kuwaiti stock market. The reason for the choice of site was its proximity to the Kuwaiti stock exchange, so that traders were constantly informed about what was going on inside the official stock exchange. The building was also near the banks, which made financial dealings between traders easier and faster. Moreover, the offices of most big merchants and investors were in the same area, as well as the head offices of several Gulf public companies, making it easy for traders and dealers to meet and obtain information about companies.

The landlord fixed a monthly rent of KD 300 for a single office, on top of a non-refundable lump sum of KD 30,000, known as *Qafliya*.[9]

Brokers and owners of property companies scrambled to obtain offices in the building, so that within no time at all, not a single office remained vacant. Signboards were erected, saying, 'For share-trading and property'. All in all, the market consisted of 16 offices engaging a total of 70 brokers;[10] some were self-employed, the others employed by companies. A typical office would contain a long counter, behind which sat a number of brokers and assistants facing several telephones on the counter. Just off the counter, on the other side, were chairs for clients. During the afternoon and evening the market was so crowded with traders that it was difficult to move between offices along the corridors. Everybody would be busy, asking questions, comparing rates and discussing, taking share cards. Some carried briefcases, but most carried chequebooks in their jackets. While Arab coffee and tea were served to clients and incense burnt, brokers would call out the share prices, either offered or bid. As they named the price, the traders decided whether to buy or sell. Unlike other stock exchanges, there were no electronic boards showing movements of prices in Al-Manakh. However, the telephones rarely stopped, and brokers and assistants would answer two telephones simultaneously, giving information or making transactions. Most of these offices were licensed for property business and share-trading, and officially recognised by both the Chamber of Commerce and the Municipality. Share-trading of Gulf companies remained an illegitimate aspect of their activities.

This was how Souq Al-Manakh started in 1978, a year which witnessed record activity in share-trading. The boom was followed by a period of serious recession which plagued the market for the best part of 1979, particularly during the last few months. The recession crept into the new year and worsened, cutting the total trading volume in 1980 by 15 per cent compared with 1979, while the total value of traded shares decreased by 28 per cent. When Souq Al-Manakh revived, 1981 and the first eight months of 1982, witnessed a trading surge which surpassed all expectations, and a steady increase in the total value of traded shares. Trading in Gulf shares reached 3,500 million shares at a face value of US$ 200m but a market value of US$ 6,000m.[11] It was a golden age, during which speculation escalated, prices rocketed, and shares multiplied, while Kuwaitis flocked to trade in a market still considered illegitimate in the eyes of government and law. The activity was unprecedented in Kuwait since the creation of public companies and the establishment of the Kuwaiti stock exchange during the 1950s. Together with the Kuwaiti stock exchange, it became third among world stock exchanges, with a volume of trading that sometimes surpassed that of London.[12]

Eventually, Al-Manakh emerged as a cornerstone of the Kuwaiti commercial structure, enjoying an autonomous status and organisation. The founders and company owners acted almost without restraint, raising and bringing down prices virtually at will. A time came when everybody was connected with or affected by Al-Manakh. However, the more the market flourished, the more chaotic transactions became.

Deferred payment deals in particular grew strikingly. The Ministry of Industry and Commerce intervened, prohibiting brokers from offering shares of any Gulf company without prior approval from the Ministry. It also obliged companies to prepare annual budgets, decreeing that any company failing to do so would be prohibited from offering its shares in the market. The contraventions persisted. By the end of 1981, the Ministry had to intervene. A consultative committee was set up, consisting of representatives of the Gulf companies, the Ministry of Commerce and Industry, the Ministry of Finance and the Chamber of Commerce and Industry. By early 1982, it had started to reorganise transactions in the market, requiring brokers' offices to show the date of every transaction, the names of buyer and seller and their signatures.[13] Copies of all transactions were sent to the Ministry at the end of the morning and evening business sessions, at 1.00 pm and 8.00 pm. In this way the Ministry was in a position to know at first hand the number of shares sold, closing prices of every company share and the nature of transactions, whether cash or deferred payment. The Ministry analysed the data and prepared a daily bulletin for publication in the newspapers which listed the company's name, minimum and maximum prices and volume of trading.[14] However such monitoring measures failed to discipline the market.

Al-Manakh's brokers were ignorant about the nature of the work of a stock exchange. Land and property brokers by origin, when share trading was introduced, they automatically changed to the new business. Moreover, they were mostly interested parties, since they took stakes in the companies they traded. Stripped of the impartiality of disinterested advisers, they promoted those companies in which they were personally interested. Their daily profit ranged from KD 6,000 to KD 100,000 or more. By the beginning of 1982, the prosperity of the market seemed to peak. The volume of trading reached fabulous proportions. The phenomenon of deferred payment transactions spread so fast that deferment periods were extended from six and twelve months to years, and the interest rate on postdated cheques reached 300 per cent.[15]

Deferred payment is a system sometimes practised in stock exchanges, particularly in futures markets. A typical transaction is for the cash price of a given share to be, say, KD 1 at a given time. The investor orders a certain number, but instead of paying in cash he gives a postdated cheque, say, for six months. The premium for the deferment is 25 per cent, so the transaction between seller and buyer closes at the share price plus 25 per cent, in this example. According to accepted practice in international stock exchanges, the shares are not acquired by the buyer until the period of deferment has expired and the cheque been paid, nor is the buyer entitled to deal in the shares. At the stock exchange in Kuwait, it was another story. Immediately after giving his postdated cheque to the seller, the buyer began to deal in the shares while the seller waited until the deferment period expired. The only guarantee of payment was mutual confidence. By the beginning of 1982, the number of such transactions had become astronomical. Exploiting the situation to the maximum, gamblers would buy shares in cash at the prevailing market price, only to re-sell them for deferred payment a year or more ahead at a profit. Though vast profits were realised, large numbers of traders were seriously affected by the collapse of the market.

Al-Manakh had become a vast gambling casino; it attracted people from all walks of life, from big businessmen and entrepreneurs to students, senior and junior officials, the military and even women, all of whom became traders in the stock market, either selling or buying, waiting for profits or employing shares for one year periods, getting buyers to deal further in them and collecting in return a postdated cheque. Crazed with fast profit-making, nobody stopped to think about the outcome. Eventually, the market attracted scores of amateurs who added to its growing dilemma.

The market made inroads into the property market. It became a normal practice for an owner of shares to barter his shares for a building or plot of land. In another transaction, a brokership might be bought by one company from another at KD 7m (US$ 20m), plus a *Qafliya* (premium) of KD 17m (US$ 50m) for a small office measuring 2m × 7m.[16] Despite the excesses, traders in the stock market remained curiously optimistic about the future of the market, believing that share prices were yet to peak, quoting the experience of the share prices of Kuwaiti incorporated companies which had, in the past, reached a level not yet attained by their Gulf counterparts. On the whole, the majority of traders seemed to look upon Al-Manakh as if it were a futures market. This may explain why speculation at Al-Manakh was the dominant activity.

The mounting scramble for quick profits further distanced the market from the impact of regulations governing the Kuwaiti stock exchange. No effective measures were taken, however, though many businessmen, officials and traders, demanded that the authorities should take a positive attitude, believing that the market's lack of official recognition was the cause of its chaotic behaviour. Others said that Al-Manakh was Kuwaiti, serving the national economy by providing an investment channel for excess liquidity. Being part and parcel of the Kuwaiti and

Gulf economic and social structure, it should not be ignored.[17]

'Abd al-'Aziz Hamad al-Saqr, Chairman of the Kuwaiti Chamber of Commerce and Industry supported the parallel market as follows:

> It is of benefit for us to transfer our activity to a second stock market under a different name, which has found no official recognition. The speciality of this market, so far, is trading shares of what are commonly known as 'Gulf public companies' — a term that we all know refers to public joint stock companies founded in the sister Arab Gulf countries by Kuwaiti initiative, and under semi-total Kuwaiti control of ownership, management and share-trading.
>
> These companies have several encouraging factors: first, they represent a trend of Kuwaiti private investment towards Arab Gulf countries, which in itself helps to consolidate their economic merger and cooperation; second, they constitute an investment outlet characteristic of geographical proximity, soundness and profitability, if directed towards a project of proven economic viability; third, they broaden the market base, which helps to alleviate the pressures of speculation in the shares of Kuwaiti companies.[18]

Al-Saqr's statement implied recognition of the legitimacy of the Gulf companies and their stock exchange, though his statement included an invitation to the Kuwaiti Ministry of Commerce to put the Gulf Stock Exchange under its control; he suggested that Gulf companies should join the Kuwaiti stock exchange or even that they should be 'Kuwaitised'. A conference was held on 14th to 16th November 1981 in Kuwait to consider studies on the development of the stock exchange in Kuwait. Participants included the Kuwaiti Chamber of Commerce and Industry, the Ministry of Commerce and Industry, the Central Bank, as well as specialists, interested parties and institutions. Most speakers expressed their pride at the development of the stock exchange in Kuwait, considering it one of the chief economic achievements of the Kuwaiti national economy. Some showed concern at the future stability of the stock market, warning against continued chaos and the practice of creating ever more companies. Specifically they called for regulation of deferred-payment transactions, and positive confrontation of the problem posed by the Al-Manakh market. There were also demands that the Government intervene in order to enforce discipline on the market.[19]

Third Stage: 1982–84

In terms of market prosperity, the 1982–84 period had no significance, except for the first half of 1982, which was a natural extension of the second period.

During the first six months of 1982, the briskness of activity in Souq Al-Manakh reached record levels. Deferred-payment transactions and speculative practices proliferated and share traders succumbed completely to market euphoria and indiscipline. Interest on deferred payments increased to 400–500 per cent for some periods.[20] The momentum continued until August, though mutual confidence in dealing had begun to subside. In August, the market collapsed, bringing everything to a tragic standstill. When the dust had settled, a hastily-formed clearance institution prepared a record of postdated cheques; the size of the debts was calculated to be about US$ 90bn.[21] A significant proportion concerned deals concluded during the first half of the year.

After August there was an anti-climax. Share trading slumped. Share prices of Gulf and Kuwait companies closed and share companies in general registered a sharp decline, in which market prices slipped sharply below face value. For example, stocks whose face value was one UAE Dirham were offered at 0.15 Dirhams, 81 per cent less. Sometimes demand for shares plummeted to nil. Little wonder that, during some periods, the volume of trading declined to zero (Table 3.1 shows the decline in market prices compared to face value for a number of Gulf companies).

The slump continued into 1983 and 1984. Sporadic modest increases in share prices were recorded but these were attributed to government decisions in the aftermath of the crisis, such as the decision for the government to buy shares so as to inject public funds into the official stock exchange. Daily price bulletins during 1983 and 1984 reflect no significant improvement in company shares.[22] The numbers of share traders declined sharply and the stock market was largely deserted. (The next chapter goes into this period in greater detail.)

Impact of Souq Al-Manakh on Economic and Social Life

Throughout its golden age, Souq Al-Manakh had a considerable impact on the economic and social life in Kuwait and, to a lesser extent, in the other Gulf countries. The effects had their negative as well as positive aspects.

The stock exchanges, both Kuwaiti and in the Gulf market, acquired — in a relatively short span of time — a leading position among the international exchanges. In the opinion of economists in Kuwait and other Gulf states, the institution of the stock exchange achieved economic goals which should not be belittled, as an instrument for the distribution of

Table 3.1: Differential Between Face and Market Value of Shares of Gulf Companies in January 1984 on Al-Manakh

Company	Share face value in nominated currency unit	Face value equivalent (Kuwaiti Fils)	Market value (Kuwaiti Fils)	Downward differential percentage
Gulf Financial Centre	US$ 0.25	75	52	31
Sharjah Group	US$ 0.25	75	59	21
Gulf Medical Projects	Dh 1	80	39	51
Fujairah Cement	Dh 1	80	68	15
Petroleum Products	Dh 1	80	60	25
Ajman Cement	Dh 1	80	60	25
Gulf Real Estate	Dh 1	80	53	34
Gulf Investment and Real Estate	Dh 1	80	60	25
United International Hotels	Dh 1	80	15	81
Bahrain and Middle East Bank	US$ 0.50	150	145	3
Pearl Investment	US$ 1	300	91	70
Ras Al-Khaimah Poultry and Fodder	US$ 1	80	44	45
Bahrain and Kuwait Investment Group	Dh 1	80	54	33
Gulf Kalankar	Dh 2	160	75	53
Gulf Cement	Dh 1	80	70	13
Umm Al-Qaiwain Cement	Dh 1	80	47	41
First Gulf Bank	Dh 10	800	Demand nil on that day	—
United Insurance	Dh 1	80	Demand nil on that day	—
Arab International Insurance	US$ 1	300	Demand nil on that day	—
Arab Company for General Investments	Dh 1	80	59	26
United Gulf Industry and Services	Dh 1	80	56	30

Note: Lack of demand caused some company share prices to undergo no change for several weeks.
Source: Share prices bulletin, 3.1.84, *Al-Watan, Al-Qabas* and *Al-Seyassah* (daily newspapers), Kuwait.

wealth.[23] Admittedly, there was foul play and chaotic conduct, but these were due primarily to the slackness of the official authorities and their reluctance to enforce any sort of legal discipline.

Nevertheless, the institution of the stock exchange played an important part in the mobilisation and direction of national savings. This resulted in the consolidation of the role of public companies as the perfect instrument to set up large-scale projects, and the consequent broadening of the base of participants in the development process. During the early stage of the stock exchange, a number of public-benefit-oriented companies emerged, such as national commercial banks and manufacturing plants, which contributed to the national economy. The stock exchange also offered an outlet for small and medium savings during its early stage, although the successive waves of speculation which later overwhelmed the market undermined its ability to carry on this role.

Not only did the stock exchange — whether the official market or the parallel one — affect the Kuwaiti economic structure, it was also affected by it. It had not developed in a vacuum, but was a natural outcome of the Kuwaiti economic structure. Moreover, the existence of a stock exchange governed by law alongside an almost lawless one, naturally attracted everybody to the latter at the expense of the former. The result was that the prosperity of Al-Manakh was the direct result of the recession in the local Kuwaiti stock market. This had the effect of undermining one of the basic functions of the local stock exchange, *i.e.* the channelling of local resources into local investment. Between 1977 and 1982, Kuwaiti capital was injected at a rapidly increased rate into Gulf companies and the official Kuwaiti Stock Exchange slumped as a result, forsaken by the investors who preferred Al-Manakh because it provided greater opportunities for quick unregulated profits. Another negative consequence of Al-Manakh was that the local Kuwaiti banks courted Gulf companies and their founders, offering them facilities and guarantees. Eventually the banks found new ways of recouping high interest rates, bypassing the existing legal restrictions by reaching a high level of interest.[24]

Foremost among the regrettable consequences of the parallel market was that it undermined several productive or potentially productive sectors. Obsessed by share trading and speculation, businessmen who owned productive businesses neglected their original calling. Several productive companies — public and private — closed down. Other negative effects on economic and social life may be summarised as follows:

1. Businessmen of good standing alienated themselves from productive

work such as import-export, construction and industry, to concentrate their abilities and resources solely in share trading, until the national economy was no longer balanced. Businessmen who invested only part of their capital in Al-Manakh could achieve in one day the equivalent of a year's profits, with the minimum of effort and hardship.

A great many productive enterprises had to close down. Owners of long-established industrial plants often had to liquidate their businesses or keep their plants in a state of idleness for long periods.[25] Setting up new productive enterprises was out of the question.

2. Large-scale trading on Al-Manakh that was subject to no official regulation, coupled with its negative relationship with the official Kuwait stock exchange, helped to create a state of inflation which posed a serious threat to the national economy.

3. By attracting people from almost all levels of the working population, Al-Manakh helped to undermine the efficiency and performance of professionals such as engineers, lawyers, and technicians, as well as senior officials, and even students. Share-trading sapped the mental and physical energies of these highly-trained young people, in a society in which few were skilled. The abundant opportunities for easy profit-making offered at Al-Manakh, and the money-oriented social standards in Kuwait, make it hard to blame these ambitious and educated young men.[26] For example, a doctor, an engineer or a university lecturer would earn a monthly salary of KD 1,000, but a less educated man could gain the same sum in less than an hour on the stock exchange. Say two doctors have graduated simultaneously; one joins a professional salaried service at a hospital, the other becomes a habitué of the stock exchange. The eventual difference in their earnings would be fantastic. Before long, the salaried doctor would decide to leave his job, sacrificing a life-time of education and training.

4. Some negative effects of Al-Manakh on economic and social life spilled over to other Gulf countries, particularly the UAE and Bahrain. This was partly because Gulf companies were incorporated in those countries, and partly because a number of Gulf nationals became involved with these companies as share subscribers and traders, which automatically drew them into the activities of Souq Al-Manakh, such as monitoring its development, and dealing with brokers. As in Kuwait, numerous young men left their jobs to take up share-trading full-time. Some even started share-trading offices.

The Stock Market in Bahrain — Emergence and Development

The stock market in Bahrain underwent different and gradual stages of development. Its beginning may have been similar to Kuwait's but it developed only slowly. Bahrain's stock market was not an independent structure, and did not evolve into a modern and systematic stock exchange like the Kuwaiti one. The pace of economic development in Bahrain was slow, capital requirements modest and the island's economic resources meagre. The process of capital formation was, inevitably, weak.

The stages of development of the Bahrain stock market may be divided as follows: first stage, 1957–70; second stage, 1970–78; third stage, 1978–82.

First Stage: 1957–70 — Foundation and Growth

When pioneers from the private sector established the first national public joint-stock company in 1957, the National Bank of Bahrain, limited trading began. Over a period of thirteen years, six public joint-stock companies were founded under Emiri Decrees, with paid-up capital of BD 3,475,000 — distributed among 347,500 shares of BD 10.[27] This period was characterised by:

1. Small volume of shares issued.
2. Virtual monopoly of shares by the financially well off.
3. Poor investment consciousness among most nationals.
4. Intervention by the Government to support companies, which covered the value of all shares not acquired by public subscription.[28]

Such growth as there was helped to create awareness and enthusiasm among investors for the establishment of more joint-stock companies.

Second Stage: 1970–78 — Development and Growth of an Elementary Market

During this period, the pace of economic and social development quickened, particularly with the emergence, after national independence, of new economic institutions. This was the period of the oil boom when oil production and prices spiralled, after 1973. Government spending increased vastly, with a knock-on effect in the private sector.[29]

Investment awareness grew steadily. Ten companies were established in the financial sector, in insurance, commercial and hotel services and industry, with paid-up capital of BD 18,250,000.[30] This was the period when Kuwait grew strong in the property market. The result was that prices shot up in this sector, drawing share companies with them, where profits soared as a result of the property boom which began in 1973 and continued into 1976. Towards November and December 1976, property prices were forced down by speculation; the sharp drop in share prices in Kuwait in 1977 further pulled down land prices in Bahrain. The downward trend continued through 1978–79 although demand for new issues remained constant, so the period was characterised by more active share trading than usual.[31]

In 1975, Decree No. 28/1975 laid down the legal foundation for general joint-stock companies to issue shares and bills, methods of subscription, rights of shareholders, and procedures for buying and selling shares.[32]

By the beginning of 1975, a system of offshore banking units was set up which helped to make Bahrain a prestigious financial centre in the Arab Gulf and the Middle East.[33] The development influenced the local stock market, which prospered. Demand for financial assets and subscription to share companies increased to the point that coverage of subscriptions would amount to five times the volume of each fresh share issue.

The demand for subscriptions, though relatively big, was generally tempered by a moderation, so there was no sharp increase in share prices, no large-scale speculation and no deferred payment transactions.

In 1978, the first forerunner of the Gulf public companies was founded by Kuwaiti investors — al-Jazira Contracting.[34]

Third Stage: 1978–82 — Emergence of the Gulf Public Company and Impact of Souq Al-Manakh

During the period when new Gulf public companies proliferated, demand for their shares and for the shares of locally incorporated companies was brisk. Gulf companies — or 'exempted' companies — are a unique type of company based in Bahrain. Although they conduct business abroad, they are prohibited from doing so inside Bahrain apart from certain types of commercial business subject to licensing from the Minister of Commerce and Agriculture. They are permitted, however, to subscribe shares in Bahrain and to issue stock or negotiable securities. The concept of exempted companies may have arisen from the experiment of offshore banks. The Ministry of Commerce and Agriculture made a careful study of the implications of this type of company, an analysis which covered the possibility of undesirable competition with national companies, likely benefits and what resources were available in Bahrain for the new companies. On the basis of the findings, Resolution No. 25/1977, on the licensing of exempted companies, was issued.[35] The choice of Bahrain by owners of exempted companies, was based on geographic and economic factors, availability of manpower and services.

Scores of Kuwaiti investors descended on Bahrain intent on benefiting from a Resolution that regularised the establishment of the type of company which came to be known as a Gulf public company. Four local companies were founded during this period and their shares offered for public subscription during 1980–81. Three failed to gain sufficient coverage and went to the Gulf countries for capital. The Bahraini government did cover what remained of the shares of the third company, and the fourth was given total coverage of its shares. The combined capital of these four companies amounted to BD 69.7m.[36]

In March 1978, the first two exempted companies were launched: Gulf and Riyad Bank with capital of US$ 8m, followed by the Frab Bank (Middle East) with capital of US$ 5m. Further exempted companies were established, bringing the total for 1978 to seventeen. The number of exempted companies registered at the Ministry of Commerce and Agriculture amounted to 20 in 1979, 35 in 1980 and 78 in 1981.[37] Their business activities were concentrated in banking, finance, investment, management consultancy, property and industrial enterprises.

Decree No. 23/1981 (amending section 279 of the company law) allowed Bahrainis to become co-founders or public subscribers in Gulf shareholding companies.[38] Both Bahrainis and the stock market benefited. With share values as low as 100 fils, which brought in investors on fixed incomes, the volume of trading increased. Traders favoured both Gulf companies and locally incorporated companies, particularly after local companies created split share issues. Gulf companies had the edge, because of the relatively low value of their shares, and their association with the Kuwaiti finance markets.

Brokers dealt in shares of local companies and Gulf companies. The commercial complex where they began to gather came to be known as *Souq Al-Johara*, the jewel market. It was an unofficial market, not subject to supervision by government authority any more than its brokers were subject to official control.[39]

Al-Johara helped to create more activity in the Bahrain market between share traders and banks. Its connections with Al-Manakh in Kuwait were close, and it is even said that it was Kuwaiti investors who originally established Al-Johara along the lines of Al-Manakh as a meeting place for traders in which intelligence and information about buying and selling could be exchanged. The two exchanges resembled one another. Like Al-Manakh, Al-Johara, developed its relationships with merchants and brokers in other Gulf countries, especially in the UAE, following the interests of the founders and subscribers of Gulf companies into Bahrain, Kuwait and the UAE. Saudi Arabian and other Gulf interests were also involved.

According to figures released by the Bahrain Monetary Institution (the Central Bank) during that period, monetary liquidity rose considerably, doubling between 1979 and 1983 from BD 411m to BD 843m, with percentage rises of more than 27 and 29 per cent in 1980 and 1981 respectively. Credit facilities rose to four times the volume between 1979 and 1983, from BD 41m to BD 128m.[40] Most of these facilities were employed on the stock exchange, as there was no other place to absorb and channel them into the productive or services sectors.

Like Al-Manakh, the Bahrain stock market experienced sharp increases in share prices, which reached abnormal heights. The same applied to speculation, as Bahrainis rushed to invest. In the midst of this, Kuwaitis sought to acquire shares in new companies allotted to Bahraini nationals, by buying nationality certificates and passports at prices up to BD 20 or 30. Some traders used deferred payment, a practice until then unknown in the Bahrain stock market. However, that was during the boom period when market activity reached its peak. Share prices were shooting up irrationally, without logical connection with the actual or expected performance of companies. Neither buying nor selling was based on objective premises. Many Bahrainis acquired fairly large fortunes from share trading. Some Kuwaiti investors established links between their offices in Kuwait and brokers' offices in Bahrain. Others opened branches in Bahrain to facilitate direct dealings with Al-Manakh in Kuwait, which had the effect of connecting Al-Johara and brokers' offices elsewhere in Bahrain directly to Al-Manakh, where prices were finally fixed and transactions completed either in cash or by deferred payment. There were good working relationships between brokers in both markets, with telephone contacts continuing non-stop throughout working hours. The typical Bahraini investor was cautious and shunned risk-trading; he would buy the shares of Gulf companies newly established in Bahrain at the normal price, and sell them through the brokers of the Bahraini Stock Market at the stock market in Kuwait, at the price fixed there[41] (which may have been double the value). As prices rose in Al-Manakh, the Bahrain stock market was affected.

While it is true that long-established local companies were responsible for the creation of the Bahraini stock market, its real development and growth happened after 1979; prosperity did not come until 1981–82, a period marked by the prosperity of Al-Manakh and the creation of Gulf companies in Bahrain itself. The prosperity extended to all sectors of economic activity in Bahrain, injecting vitality into the goods, services and property markets. Founders of Gulf companies and men with a high profile at Al-Manakh used their contacts with Bahrain to obtain licences to found new companies there: a Gulf company established in Bahrain would have a better reputation than one established elsewhere in the Gulf,[42] because of the country's body of company law.

The prospering Bahrain stock market represented for Kuwaiti investors a third domain, after Kuwait and the UAE, and a second one if viewed as a semi-organised market after Al-Manakh. Far from matching Al-Manakh in size, still less in competition with it because of its smaller resources in finance and manpower, the Bahrain stock market was like a foreign branch of Al-Manakh. The advanced economic structure of Kuwait, its vast annual oil revenues and powerful business community, gave the Kuwaiti finance market seniority in the markets of the Gulf region and the Middle East.

The prosperity of the Bahrain market was so dependent on that of Al-Manakh that when collapse overtook Al-Manakh the catastrophe spilt over into the Bahrain market. All investors suffered, large and small. The small investors in particular had taken out bank loans secured by their property or by the personal guarantee of a relative with a current bank account. The extent of the catastrophe in the Johara Market was, therefore, tremendous: 'the Jewel' was now valueless. Unaccustomed to such catastrophic losses, the average Bahraini share trader felt profoundly affected, though less so than his Kuwaiti counterparts. There is no accurate statistical data on the extent to which Bahrain share traders were involved in the catastrophe of Al-Manakh; according to reports released by the institution for the settlement of deferred payment transactions in Kuwait, Bahraini involvement ranged between BD 25m and 35m, in the form of Kuwaiti postdated cheques. By Bahraini standards that was a colossal figure, and could seriously undermine the financial position of any of those Bahraini investors whose names were included in the list of Al-Manakh victims.[43] At the time of the crash, 90 per cent of the shares of the Gulf companies were Kuwaiti owned.

Although individuals in Bahrain incurred relatively little damage, substantial damage was done to the economy. Shares of local companies suffered too, because the Al-Manakh crisis coincided with internal and external developments which caused an outflow of money to be deposited in foreign banks abroad.

As a small oil producer with limited resources for economic development, Bahrain had encouraged the establishment of local companies, 'exempted' companies and offshore banking units in a bid to diversify and increase its sources of income, so it joined in the efforts to revive the stock market in the aftermath of the crash. Conferences and seminars were convened to examine the structure of the stock market, restore life to the market and inject greater vigour into the economy.

The market improved every time new measures were announced in Kuwait. The volume of trading in February 1983, for example, amounted to more than eight million shares, out of which 1.4 million belonged to local companies, and 6.6 million to Gulf companies. In April, the value of both Gulf and local company shares rose — in some cases by 100 per cent. For example, the share price of the National Bank of Bahrain shot up from BD 6 to BD 13. The daily volume of trading jumped from zero in March and April 1983 to more than fifty thousand by June,[44] all this at a time when the aftermath of the Al-Manakh fall in Kuwait was yet to be resolved. At the end of June, share prices at Al-Johara dropped abruptly by 50 per cent. The downward trend continued until prices reached the low crisis level of Al-Manakh. Some people attributed the drop to the March fall in crude oil prices, when the Organisation of Oil Exporting Countries (OPEC) had agreed to slash the reference price for oil by five dollars to US$ 29 a barrel. They argued that the drop in oil prices took time to filter through and affect share prices. Others said that share prices had climbed in May and June because the banks and the government made loans to Bahraini investors to enable them to buy shares at Al-Manakh. However, due to failure on the part of Kuwaiti investors to make good their postdated cheques made payable to Bahraini share traders following the Al-Manakh collapse, the Bahrainis also defaulted on their bank loans. They took shares as part-payments for loans, and the share prices of some companies rose; but the banks acquired no more shares and share prices returned to former levels. The exercise demonstrated that share value, especially shares in 'exempted' Gulf companies trading locally, was intimately linked to fluctuations at Al-Manakh in Kuwait.[45]

A seminar on the Bahrain stock market was convened on 1st May 1984 in Manamah, to discuss papers presented by the Ministry of Commerce and Agriculture and the Bahraini Chamber of Commerce on the market's crisis and problems. A scheme for an official stock exchange was put forward, and an ad hoc committee to study the scheme was set up, comprising membership from the Ministry of Commerce and Agriculture, the Ministry of Finance and National Economy, the Bahraini Monetary Institution, and the Chamber of Commerce. The committee asked the International Finance Corporation (IFC) of the International

Bank for Reconstruction and Development (IBRD) to prepare a feasibility study of the existing state of the stock market, and to make concrete proposals for developing the market. The IFC's report backed a proposal for an official Bahrain stock exchange on both economic and social grounds, and the Ministry of Commerce and Agriculture took preliminary steps to establish a modern stock exchange. A centre of information for brokers and share traders was set up as a transitional step. The centre was equipped with four direct telephone lines, so that through brokers registered with the Ministry data could be rapidly exchanged and put on the teletype machines. Though modest, the innovation was adequate at the time.[46] It was seen as a step in the right direction, demonstrating that Bahrain intended to develop and organise its stock market, prior to resolving all the dilemmas of share trading. It was hoped the move would encourage the demand for shares and prepare the market for the time when Al-Manakh and the Kuwaiti stock exchange would recover and return to normal activity.

Bahrain's stock market occupied second place, after Kuwait, in terms of an organisation that was semi-regularised, whose brokers were licensed and subject to supervision by a government body (the Ministry of Commerce and Agriculture). Judged by volume of trading, Bahrain came third, after the disorganised stock market in the UAE.

Table 3.2: Bahraini Public Companies 1957–81

Name	Year of incorporation	Paid-up capital at the time of subscription	Paid-up capital at 31.12.83 (BD)
National Bank of Bahrain	1957	125,000	28,000,000
Ship Repairs	1962	800,000	800,000
National Insurance	1967	500,000	1,000,000
Bahrain Cinema	1967	500,000	1,500,000
Bahrain Hotels	1967	1,500,000	8,484,480
Bahrain Insurance	1969	150,000	600,000
Bank of Bahrain and Kuwait	1971	1,000,000	30,874,000
National Hotels	1973	1,500,000	14,000,000
Flour Mills	1973	400,000	1,600,000
Import	1973	1,000,000	4,000,000
Bahrain Tourism	1974	1,100,000	7,134,640
Bahraini Kuwaiti Insurance	1975	500,000	1,200,000
National Commercial Bank	1977	4,000,000	8,000,000
General Foods	1977	2,500,000	2,500,000
Bahraini Islamic Bank	1979	5,750,000	5,750,000
Delman Poultry	1980	1,500,000	2,906,126
Light Industries	1980	1,176,780	2,500,000
Car Parks	1981	7,032,000	7,031,723
Bahrain Telecommunications	1981	60,000,000	60,000,000
Total		91,033,780	187,881,469

Source: Department of Commerce and Company Affairs, Ministry of Commerce and Agriculture, 1982.

Stock Market in the United Arab Emirates (UAE)

By the beginning of the 1960s, Dubai had emerged as an important commercial centre, built on the extraction of crude oil in Abu Dhabi. Searching for new outlets for their savings, investors began to set up public companies, which rapidly became an important sector of the national economy. The stock market which emerged and developed in the process passed through three stages of growth: first stage, 1962–71; second stage, 1971–76; third stage, 1976–84.

First Stage: 1962–71

Crude oil marked the end of traditional economic occupations in the Emirates, which had depended on commerce, fishing and the pearl trade. The stage was set for serious economic development which demanded reform of the existing economic structure and the establishment of a modern infrastructure. The Emirate of Dubai took the initiative in economic development and diversification before the oil era, because of its geographical position as a transit centre for the gold trade between Europe and the Indian sub-continent. The privileges given to business had also created a flourishing domestic economy. The leading merchants had close contacts with their counterparts in Kuwait, Bahrain and India.[47] In addition to goods, the Dubai merchants also brought back ideas, one of which was the public company. The pioneers were the large merchants who, led by Sayyid 'Ali Abdallah al-'Uwaysi, set up the National Bank of Dubai in 1963, the country's first public company, with capital of 13.5m Rupees.[48] Only a limited number of nationals shared in the equity with Sayyid 'Ali, but among those who took a stake from outside were the Kuwaiti National Bank and the British Bank. The existence of the bank allowed the Emirates, and particularly Dubai, to handle the first negotiable bill of its type. The Dubai Electricity Company, which had been established on 18th May 1959 with 3m Rupees capital, was more of a closed than a public company, since the equity was shared between the government of Dubai and a limited number of individuals.[49] (The company was nationalised by the Government of Dubai on 1st January 1980 and the shareholders compensated.) Encouraged by the discovery of oil and the consequent expansion of the commercial sector, the success shown by the National Bank of Dubai, the relative growth in the volume of liquidity and by the high price of land, investors began to establish more public companies. The Bank of Oman opened in 1967 but, though a number of other companies followed, they were more in the nature of closed than public companies.

In 1969 the Dubai Commercial Bank Ltd was founded, followed in 1970 by the Dubai Bank Ltd.[50]

With the exception of Abu Dhabi, the Emirates had no public companies.[51] Although the export of oil had begun as early as 1962, the leading public company in Abu Dhabi, the National Bank of Abu Dhabi, was not founded until 1968. The shareholders were the Abu Dhabi investment authority, which took 61.9 per cent, and UAE individuals who took the remaining 38.1 per cent.[52]

In the Emirate of Sharjah, the first public company to be established was Sharjah Insurance in 1970, in which the Government of Sharjah took a stake.[53] The company was incorporated in 1979 as a Gulf company, with Kuwaiti participation. Public companies like these were established before national independence came to the Emirates. Their pre-independence characteristics were:

1. Negligible volume of shares issued.
2. Concentration on finance-investment companies, especially on banks.
3. Virtual monopoly of share ownership by wealthy merchants, with a percentage set aside for the government of the Emirate (in some cases, this went to one family).
4. Novelty. Local investors had little knowledge of financial assets in the current sense. These companies showed striking success and yielded huge annual profits; and, since the only shares that were bought were limited in number, neither share trading nor speculation occurred.[54]
5. The overriding reason for putting money into these companies was that they represented vehicles for long-term investment.

Second Stage: 1971–76. The Post-Independence Period

This period witnessed the creation of the federal political structure which brought all the Emirates together under the umbrella of the United Arab Emirates on 2nd December 1971. New economic institutions were created to implement a comprehensive programme of economic and social development. The need for a modern infrastructure led to a surge of prosperity in all sectors, in the wake of the oil boom of 1973 when the state's revenues doubled several times in a few years.[55] The flow of liquidity encouraged the establishment of more companies and banks. The growth of relations with the outside world was another encouraging incentive. There was a rush to establish what, at first sight, were multi-purpose companies, which transpired to be no more than banks, because these were relatively easy to establish and offered almost guaranteed profitability. During this period alone twelve banks were started in different Emirates.[56] Despite the existence of the 'Currency Board', which was created on independence to represent the federal monetary authority which alone was entrusted with the power to grant licences for new banks, individual Emirates granted licences unilaterally, or put pressures on the Board to do so.

Several companies in various fields were established in the seventies. Emirates Telecommunications Ltd, (EMIRTEL) established under an Emiri Decree No. 78/1976 with capital of 200m Dirhams, concentrated on telephone and other communications services; 40 per cent of its shares were offered by the government for public subscription.[57] The Government of Abu Dhabi also helped to establish the Abu Dhabi Hotels Company in 1976 with capital which amounted to 100m Dirhams; 35 per cent of its shares were owned by the government of Abu Dhabi, 65 per cent were offered by the Government for public subscription by UAE nationals. Some insurance companies were established, as well as the Al-Ain Cement plant, the Sharjah Cement plant (which became known in 1979 as a Gulf company), and the Union Cement plant at Ras Al-Khaimah.[58] Though the Emirates and individuals showed marked activity in setting up new companies, convinced as they were of their profitability, the individual tended to follow the lead of his Emirate. For example, individual investors in the Emirates of Abu Dhabi and Dubai were relatively ahead in the establishment of companies, while the Emirate of Sharjah came third and other Emirates lagged behind.

Generally speaking, this period was characterised by:

1. The promulgation of laws and regulations which allowed companies to extend their sphere of activity to more than one Emirate simultaneously.
2. A growing awareness among individuals of the importance of public companies as investment channels, though banks headed the league because they were easy to set up and offered secure profits.
3. The creation of a specialised government authority at federal level, the Ministry of Economics and Commerce. This federal body was weak and confined to the sectors of commerce, companies and commercial agencies, since the influence of individual Emirates was, for all practical purposes, more effective than that of the federal authorities.
4. The emergence of the company share as a stable financial asset, one of the best bills of exchange, and able to shield its bearer from inflation. Bearers enjoyed reasonable and steady profits.

5. Investment consciousness which remained below optimum, thwarting the appearance of a fully-fledged stock market and confining trading within limited margins (and at reasonable prices).

There was little speculation, since people's expectations were based on company performance not on share trading. Moreover, no figures were available on numbers of shares traded or average prices, since transactions were mostly rudimentary, direct and within narrow limits.[59]

Third Stage: 1976–84. Emergence of Gulf Companies

The continuation of economic and social development in the United Arab Emirates brought about by the oil boom not only produced share companies and encouraged people to subscribe to their shares, but made the companies themselves an important sector of the national economy. The period saw uninterrupted progress in different sectors of the economy, not just the oil sector. As oil revenues multiplied, national savings as a percentage of GNP rose from 53 per cent in 1975 to 54.7 per cent in 1980; national savings sustained steady annual growth of 16.8 per cent during this period.[60] However, although governments and individuals invested, no systematic development at federal level was ever undertaken, though the Ministry of Planning had worked out a five year plan (theoretically extending to 1985) which was never carried out. Semi-chaos resulted and projects overlapped.

Some people thought that the distribution of wealth was unjust, both horizontally and vertically. They saw that wealth was concentrated in the Emirates endowed with high oil production, or in a unique commercial position. Ignoring the social services provided by the federal authority, they observed that those in the less privileged Emirates were driven to endlessly prospecting for investment outlets, largely unassisted by their ill-funded governments. Such people, the argument went, were no less ambitious than their fellow citizens in the rich Emirates.

The result was an economic landscape in chaos. Each Emirate had its independent economic and commercial system, and each Emirate was the final licensing authority for any enterprise within its borders. Of course, regional autonomy to a certain degree was legitimate and desirable within a federal system of government, but not to the extent of neutralising the powers of the federal authority. In the UAE the need for overall coordination between the Emirates in the field of economic development was particularly strongly felt.[61] A discussion of economic development in the UAE is outside the scope of this study, but as it has a direct bearing on investment in joint-stock public companies and the stock market, some comment is needed.

The most significant development during this period was the emergence of Gulf companies founded by Kuwaiti investors under licences issued, not by the federal authority but by local Emirates. The flow of Kuwaiti capital was a direct result of the Kuwaiti government's ban on licences for new companies.[62] According to figures given by the UAE Association of Chambers of Commerce, the total number of public companies during this period was over 70: banks, insurance companies, industrial companies, property companies, investment and services companies, joint ventures between government and the private sector, and Gulf companies established with joint Kuwaiti and local capital. Of this latter group,[63] the first Gulf company came into being in 1976 in the Emirate of Sharjah (the Sharjah Group). Others followed, all based on the northern Emirates. None was established in Abu Dhabi, and only one in Dubai, the Arab Company for General Investments, *Shua'a*. By 1982, the total number of Gulf companies — industrial, investment, manufacturing and insurance — was 35, distributed as follows:[64]

Ajman	:	11
Ras Al-Khaimah	:	10
Sharjah	:	9
Fujairah	:	2
Umm Al-Qaiwain	:	2
Dubai	:	1
Total		35

With the exception of two banks, the companies had nothing to do with the federal authorities. Bank of the Arab Coast in Ras Al-Khaimah, and First Gulf Bank in Ajman were, of course, linked to the Central Bank.

As Gulf companies appeared and their shares were being traded at the Al-Manakh stock exchange in Kuwait, an unofficial stock market began to develop in the UAE. Brokers' offices had been springing up in some of the Emirates since 1979, and dealing in both local and Gulf company shares. The Emirate of Sharjah was the pioneer in organised mass share trading through brokers' offices. Afterwards, offices were opened in Ajman, Ras Al-Khaimah and Dubai. Abu Dhabi was apathetic at first, but it was not long before the Emirate's merchants began to realise the profitability of share trading, and opened brokers' offices in Abu Dhabi.

Brokers' offices in the UAE as a whole were connected to the stock market in Kuwait and subject to its influence. On the other hand, the UAE's inexperienced investors were no match for Kuwaiti investors, so share prices of Gulf companies owned by UAE nationals came to be fixed at Al-Manakh. It is estimated that UAE shares were traded at Al-Manakh at 20 to 30 times earnings and roughly four times book value.[65] A UAE broker only needed to obtain a 'shares and real estate' commercial licence from the municipality in order to open an office; otherwise he was subject to no law or regulation, either at federal or local level, unless he operated in Sharjah and came under the provisions of its brokers' law No. 1/1981 (see Chapter 2).

Brokers' offices were scattered throughout the town and conducted their business largely by telephone. Each broker kept notes of clients' orders to buy or sell. Brokers themselves were mostly ignorant about the companies in whose shares they were trading and so were not in a position to give professional advice. They made no recommendations and did not solicit orders. Rather than acting as a principal himself or involving another broker, a broker generally acted as a go-between on an agency basis between two investors. Once a transaction was agreed, settlement was arranged. The broker would either go himself or send a messenger to the seller to collect the stock certification and obtain the seller's signature renouncing ownership in the shares. At the same time, a messenger or the broker himself would go to the buyer and collect a cheque made out to the seller. Commission was settled from the transaction at half a per cent of transaction value,[66] although sometimes less was charged.

Although trading was not subject to regulation, the local stock market experienced an upsurge of activity throughout 1981 and the first half of 1982, which was a reflection of the frenzied activity at Al-Manakh in Kuwait. The market in the UAE responded, resulting in ever bigger deals and faster cycles of buying and selling. Meanwhile, it became evident that many Gulf companies incorporated in the UAE existed only on paper;[67] (*e.g.* Gulf Animal Resources in Ajman, and Emirates Kalankar in Fujairah).

The impact of Al-Manakh on the irregular stock market in the UAE was multi-sided. First, numerous UAE nationals, particularly in the northern Emirates, enjoyed large cash benefits. They were not speculators nor big owners of shares, as the Kuwaitis were, but they sold whenever they found what they judged was a reasonable price. Governments which had granted establishment licences to the companies benefited because they acquired a substantial proportion of shares which were traded at Al-Manakh for cash or deferred payments. Although speculation had been unknown in the stock market in the UAE during the first years, the spectacle of quick profit-making at Al-Manakh persuaded many to get involved in deferred-payment transactions. Some traders bought local company shares by deferred payment and at high prices, though this was within narrow limits. UAE nationals also used deferred payments to sell to investors in Kuwait, at high prices and for periods of three, six or twelve months. When Al-Manakh collapsed, UAE nationals were dragged with it, either through buying high and not being able to dispose of the shares when the collapse occurred, or by selling post-dated cheques which never become due. After the crash, a committee was set up in the UAE under the presidency of the Chairman of the Federation of Chambers of Commerce and comprising members of the Chambers of Commerce and affected local investors, to calculate cheques due by Kuwaiti investors. The committee assessed the total value of the cheques due in 1982 to be 500m Dirhams, but it is thought that the real figure was greater because several businessmen of repute, officials and members of ruling families had probably not presented their cheques.[68] It caused no surprise that most of the affected traders were from the northern Emirates, the majority of whom had secured large bank loans to guarantee coverage of postdated cheques. The committee president met Kuwaiti officials to discuss the interests of their nationals, and many holders of postdated cheques secured repayment.

Official Stock Exchange Scheme

While Al-Manakh stock exchange was still a major concern in Kuwait and throughout the Gulf, the United Arab Emirates announced a scheme for a local stock exchange. A high-level commission was set up, with members drawn from the Association of Chambers of Commerce, the Central Bank, Commercial Banks, the Ministry of Finance and Industry, the Ministry of Economics and Trade, and the Municipalities Secretariat and Investment Funds. Subsequently a technical committee was set up consisting of representatives of four bodies: the Association of Chambers of Commerce, the Ministry of Economics and Trade, the Central Bank and the Department of *Fatwa* and Legislation.[69]

The purpose behind the stock exchange scheme was to safeguard the smooth growth of the economy. The feasibility study was favourable. The main conclusion was that the UAE satisfied the prerequisites for a fully-fledged stock exchange, especially since there already existed more than 70 public companies as well as banks, insurance companies and a variety of Gulf public companies incorporated in the country.

The stock exchange was to be an independent legal entity in the form of a public corporation enjoying financial and administrative autonomy. The stock exchange would eventually employ an automated computerised system, preceded by a transitional stage involving the establishment of a nerve centre connected to a telephone network. The feasibility report was optimistic that the stock exchange would encourage both a primary (issuing) and secondary (trading) market, and contribute to the growth of individual savings. Moreover, it would help encourage share traders to resume activity,[70] after the confidence-shaking ordeal of Al-Manakh.

The headquarters of the stock exchange corporations was to be at Abu Dhabi. The stock market itself was to form a network covering Abu Dhabi, Dubai and Sharjah; it was thought that other Emirates would join later, and the UAE exchange would probably become linked to stock exchanges in other GCC countries. The Commission was appointed in November 1982. June 1983 was set as the operational date for the stock exchange, but the draft ordinance has not — up to the time of writing — been worked out by the technical committee. The draft ordinance was studied by the Higher Technical Committee which referred it to the Minister of Finance and Industry who was supposed to submit it to the Council of Ministers so that it would pass through the legislative stages leading to its final promulgation. It is still held up somewhere, and until it becomes law the stock exchange scheme is frozen.

The Ministry of Economics and Trade prepared a draft federal law to govern the creation and performance of companies, and avert earlier mistakes in this sphere. The law was passed by the Council of Ministers and by the National Federal Assembly, and was ratified by the Supreme Federal Council. It came up on 20th March 1984.[71] Proclaimed under Law No. 8/1984, it has 15 chapters and 329 sections. It is chapter 5 which particularly interests us because it deals with public companies; its sections cover property, founding, management, accounts, shares and liquidation. In general, the law sought to provide safeguards against most of the abuses that followed the founding of public joint stock companies, especially Gulf companies. For instance, section 77 stipulated that an invitation for public subscription should be by written announcement published in two local Arab daily newspapers, at least five days before subscriptions opened. The written announcement was to include a resume of the Articles of Association and excerpts from them, a statement proclaiming that the founders had paid up the proportion of the value of shares available to nationals and instructions concerning their disposal. Section 78 stipulated that the founders should subscribe to not less than 20 per cent and not more than 45 per cent of the company's capital; and that, before publication of the subscription statement, they should pay a sum equivalent to the proportion required to be paid up by subscribers for each share; and finally that they should, prior to inviting public subscriptions, provide the Ministry with a bank statement proving that the said proportion was actually paid-up. Section 88 obliged the founders to invite subscribers of within 30 days of the closing date for subscription, and to send a copy of the invitation to the Ministry. Section 99 stated that the chairman of the board of directors should be a national. Section 100 stipulated that nationals should constitute a majority on the board. Section 153, dealing with the company's shares, required that the company's capital should consist of equal shares, the nominal value of each share being not less than 1 Dirham and not more than 100 Dirhams, and that at the founding date no shares should be issued for less than or more than the stated nominal value. Section 197 prohibited the company from granting a cash loan of any kind to the board chairman or to any board member or providing a guarantee for any loan obtained in their favour from a third party, a tactic much favoured by Gulf companies (see Chapter 2).

While Law No. 8 covered most of the previous malpractices of UAE companies not hitherto governed by the law, it did not lay down that the shareholders of public companies should all be nationals, as was the case in Kuwait. It sought, on the contrary, to recognise the *status quo*, particularly with regard to the numerous companies whose shares had already been acquired in large proportions by Kuwaitis or other Gulf citizens. The new law also did not specify the proportions of shares to be acquired by nationals, or those to be acquired by non-nationals, and mentioned simply that nationals should constitute a majority on the board of directors without fixing a specific proportion (*i.e.* more than 51 per cent). These apparent loopholes were a form of realism, without which foreign investment-seeking Emirates would not have approved of it. It left open the door for the establishment of companies with foreign capital or investors.

The law was a positive step towards the regularising of company practice. However, although it was officially proclaimed and published in the Official Gazette, the question still remained whether it would be effective, whether individual Emirates would observe it, or whether it would be worth the paper it was written on.

Notes

1. 'The Story of the Illegitimate Child who Overtook the Legitimate Sons', *Al-Watan*, 3.11.84, pp. 10–11.

2. Ibid.

3. Verbal information obtained in April 1982 from a broker who was (and is) working in the stock market.

4. 'Collapse of the Al-Manakh Empire', *Al-Khaleej*, No. 1266, 26.9.82.

5. Hazem El-Beblawi and Raid Fahmi, *The Kuwait Stock Exchange*, IBM papers, series No. 6, (Kuwait: The Industrial Bank of Kuwait, KSC, January 1982), pp. 53–4.

6. Hazem El-Beblawi and Raid Fahmi, 'Role of the Stock Market in the Kuwaiti Economy'. Paper submitted to the Conference on the Development of the Stock Market in Kuwait between 14th to 16th November 1981. (Kuwait: Kuwaiti Chamber of Commerce and Industry, 1981), p. 67.

7. Central Bank of Kuwait, *Ten Years of Kuwait's Economy*, Economic Survey, 1969–79, p. 104.

8. *Al-Watan*, 3.11.84, p. 10.

9. 'The Mysteries of the World of Gulf Shares Speculation in Kuwait', *Al Bayan*, No. 6281, 4.2.82, p. 3.

10. Ibid.

11. Riad al-Abrash, 'Phenomenon of Gulf Public Companies', paper submitted to the Conference on thè Development of the Stock Market in Kuwait between 14th and 16th November 1981, (Kuwait: Kuwaiti Chamber of Commerce and Industry, 1981), p. 398.

12. Central Bank of Kuwait, Economic Survey, 1969–79, pp. 106–8.

13. *Al-Watan*, 3.11.84, p. 10.

14. See specimens of share sale forms and press bulletins (appendix 2).

15. John Bulloch, *The Gulf*, (London: Century Publishing Ltd, 1984), p. 134.

16. 'The Mysteries of the World of Gulf Shares Speculation in Kuwait', *Al Bayan*, No. 630, 6.2.82, p. 3.

17. Seminar on Gulf Public Companies, convened during the Conference on the Development of the Stock Market in Kuwait between 14th and 16th November 1981, (Kuwait: Kuwaiti Chamber of Commerce and Industry, 1981), pp. 425–53; see also supplement on 'Gulf Public Companies', *Al Seyassah*, No. 4927, 17.3.82, pp. 21–37.

18. Extract from opening speech by Abdel Aziz Al Saqr at the Conference on the Development of the Stock Exchange in Kuwait between 14th and 16th November 1981, (Kuwait: Kuwaiti Chamber of Commerce and Industry, 1981), p. 8.

19. *Al-Iktissad Wal-Aamal*, [Beirut: monthly magazine, The Arab Press for Publishing and Information], No. 33, December 1981, p. 22.

20. 'Alī Hasan Al-Hamdān, *Kuwait and the Crisis of Souq Al-Manakh*, (Kuwait, Umm al-Qurā Bookshop, 1984), p. 49.

21. 'The Collapse of the Kuwaiti Stock Exchange of a turnover of US$ 90bn', *Washington Post*, 24.11.82.

22. *Al-Watan* and *Al Anba*, price bulletins from January 1983 to January 1984.

23. Supplement on 'Gulf Investment', *Al-Khaleej*, No. 1194, 15.7.82, p. 4.

24. Kathy Evans, 'Souk Al-Manakh problem edges towards banking doorstep', *Financial Times*, (supplement, Arab Banking 10), 15.10.84.

25. Seminar on Gulf shares, Kuwaiti Chamber of Commerce, 1981, p. 432.

26. Seminar on Gulf Shares, Kuwaiti Chamber, 1981, p. 432–3.

27. Habīb Ahmad Qāsim, Minister of Commerce and Agriculture in Bahrain, Study presented at a Seminar on 'Reality of the Stock Market in Bahrain', (Bahrain: Bahrain Chamber of Commerce and Industry, 1st May 1984).

28. *Commerce Review Magazine* [Bahrain: Bahrain Chamber of Commerce and Industry], No. 183, June/July 1981, p. 14.

29. 'Stocks in Bahrain-5', *Al-Khaleej*, 11.3.82.

30. Department of Commerce and Company Affairs Publication, (Bahrain: Ministry of Commerce and Agriculture, 1979).

31. Habīb Qāsim, 'Reality of the Stock Market in Bahrain', p. 4.

32. Study prepared by the Department of Economic Studies and Research, *Offshore Banking Units and Exempted Companies in Bahrain, 1975–82*, (Bahrain: Bahrain Chamber of Commerce and Industry, 1982), p. 13.

33. *Al-Khaleej News*, [Bahrain: newspaper], 1.11.83.

34. Report on Exempted Companies in Bahrain, prepared by the Department of Commerce and Company Affairs, (Bahrain: Ministry of Commerce and Agriculture, 21.6.81).

35. 'Resolution No. 25/1977 dealing with establishment and licensing of Exempted Share Companies, exemption from the provision of the 1975 Commercial Companies Law', (Bahrain: Ministry of Commerce and Agriculture, 1977).

36. Habīb Qāsim, 'Reality of the Stock Market in Bahrain', p. 6.

37. *Offshore Banking and Exempted Companies*, 1975–82, (Bahrain), p. 16.

38. Habīb Qāsim, 'Reality of the Stock Market in Bahrain', p. 7.

39. *Al Majalla*, [London: political magazine], No. 182, 6th–12th August 1983, p. 38.

40. *Annual Reports*, [Bahrain: Monetary Institution, 1979–82].

41. *Al Majalla*, No. 182, 6th–12th August 1983, p. 38.

42. Public Relations Committee, paper presented to the Seminar on 'Reality of the Stock Market in Bahrain', (Bahrain: Bahrain Chamber of Commerce and Industry, 1st May 1984), p. 5.

43. Habīb Qāsim, 'Reality of the Stock Market', (Bahrain, 1984), p. 3.

44. *Al-Khaleej*, No. 1692, 30.11.83, p. 7.

45. *Al Majalla*, No. 182, 6th–12th August 1983, p. 38–9.

46. Habīb Qāsim, 'Reality of the Stock Market in Bahrain', p. 15.

47. R.G. Fenelon, *The United Arab Emirates, an Economic and Social Survey*, second edn. (London and New York: Longman Group Ltd, 1976), pp. 65–7.

48. Written information obtained from the manager of the National Bank of Dubai, March 1985.

49. *Dubai Electricity Company*, [Dubai: Emirates Printing Press, 1984]; Statement from the Dubai Government.

50. *The MEED*, Middle East Financial Directory, 1983. [London: Middle East Economic Digest in association with the National Bank of Abu Dhabi], pp. 198–201.

51. R.G. Fenelon, *The UAE*, p. 65.

52. *The MEED*, 1983, p. 193.

53. Emiri Decree No. 19/1970 issued by the Ruler of Sharjah on 8.3.70; and Emiri Decree No. 68/1979, issued on 14.11.79.

54. *Annual Reports*, for the National Bank of Dubai, Dubai Commercial Bank and Sharjah Insurance Company for the years 1965–70.

55. Ragaei El-Mallakh, *Economic Development of the United Arab Emirates*, (London: Croom Helm, 1981), pp. 88–9.

56. *The MEED*, 1983, pp. 186–811.

57. Emiri Decree No. 78/1976, *Official Gazette*, No. 41, 1976.

58. Shareholding Companies in the UAE, (UAE: Information published by the UAE Federation Chambers of Commerce and Industry, 1982).

59. M. Frank Venerso, 'Stock Market Development in the UAE', preliminary Draft of Report, 7th June 1982.

60. *Al Tijara* magazine [Sharjah: Sharjah Chamber of Commerce and Industry], Nos. 1 and 2, January and February 1983, p. 39.

61. Kāmil Al-Rīhān, 'Economic prospects for the UAE 1980–85', paper delivered to the Seminar on Future of the UAE, *Al Tijara*, (1 and 2), January and February 1983, p. 43.

62. See chapter 2, p. 20–1.

63. Shareholding Companies in the UAE (UAE Federation Chambers, 1982).

64. See table 2.1.
65. Frank Venerso, 'Stock Market Development in UAE'.
66. Interim Report, 'United Arab Emirates, Securities Market. Alternative Market Mechanisms', 24th March 1983.
67. See chapter 2, pp. 24, 33–4.
68. *Al Majalla*, No. 182, 6th–12th August 1983, p. 39; and *Al-Itihad*, [UAE: newspaper], 27.10.82.
69. *Al Majalla*, No. 182, 6th–12th August 1983, p. 39.
70. Ibid, p. 40; Frank Venerso, 'Stock Market Development in UAE'.
71. 'Federal Law No. 18/1984, Reading the Trading Companies', (Abu Dhabi: Presidential Court, 20.3.84); and published in the *Official Gazette*, No. 137, April 1984, p. 7.

4

Gulf Stock Exchange Crisis

Gulf Crisis: The First of its Kind?

In the aftermath of the Souq Al-Manakh financial crash in Kuwait in August 1982, the recurring question both inside and outside the Gulf region was: could the catastrophe have been averted? But the fundamental questions are: Why was it allowed to happen? Was this crisis the first of its kind? Or did financial history give precedents?

The most famous crisis was the Wall Street Crash of 1929. During the period 1921–1929, US investors rushed into a spate of speculation which resulted in share prices soaring. The rise came to an end in 1929, the year of the Great Depression in the US economy. The stock exchange of that era was known as the rush market. There was intensive demand by investors for shares of companies about which they knew very little, producing commodities which the investors could not define. The situation was fraught with danger. This description applies to a great extent to the behaviour of investors buying shares on Al-Manakh — a similarity sufficient for the Kuwaiti crisis to be seen not as a new experience but as an old phenomenon.[1]

The policy of *laissez-faire* towards private enterprise is an established tradition in the Gulf States, both at government and popular level. It became so deeply entrenched that it created a fever of business activity motivated by greed on the part of individuals and corporations. Speculation in shares became the leading investment activity — if not the only one. The dangers should not have gone unnoticed by the government.

On the subject of the stock exchange, Lord Keynes said:

The speculators on the stock exchange could be of no harm if they

> were no more than bubbles on a flowing river of investment. However, the situation would become fraught with danger if investment itself turned into bubbles on a whirlpool of speculation. When capital growth in any country becomes a by-product of gambling activity, the stock exchange role becomes negative.[2]

That was exactly the case with the Gulf stock exchange, Souq Al-Manakh, which was based on a working mechanism which consisted of three main components:

1. A wave of exaggerated optimism on the part of investors about the future of share prices, which was reflected in inflated prices.
2. Almost no connection between information on the shares and the decision to buy.
3. Easily available finance through payment by postdated cheques, backed up by banking facilities on a huge scale.

As a result, Al-Manakh became a market for forward buying on a vast scale, where speculation relied on the investors' anticipation that share prices would go up. Normally in such a market, optimism and pessimism balance out until actual share value is close to market value. That happened recently on the Al-Manakh exchange, where the market value of some companies' shares dropped below their real value.

In this chapter we shall discuss the causes of the crisis, both direct and indirect; the intervention by the government; and the aftermath of the crisis till the time of writing.

Start of the Crisis

All indications pointed to imminent financial crisis. Some market analysts and observers expected it at any time in view of the absence of all controls and standards: the stock exchange had become a gambling casino. Others foresaw the crisis occurring in December 1982, the date when many of the postdated cheques fell due. However, as early as July of the same year the market began to tumble. Business confidence began to waver as traders presented cheques prior to the date they were payable, so as to meet their urgent need for liquidity after the banks had refused to extend further cash facilities. During that month share prices began to fall, but the situation still seemed under control and some traders managed to cover themselves. But already traders' failure to honour their obligations shook a money market where trading was based on confidence. Nothing seemed to hold together any more. Throughout July, the crisis gathered momentum. In August, it broke. One of the major traders, a well-known business woman, presented a cheque for KD 55m to the bank, expecting it to be cashed at a discount before the date it became due. The law in Kuwait allows banks to honour a postdated cheque before it is due provided the drawer has enough credit to cover it. The cheque was drawn by Jāsim al-Mutawwa', one of the big speculators, who had bartered the lady's shares in Ajman Cement for property she owned, leaving a balance of KD 55m, in settlement of which he had made out a cheque.[3] She presented the cheque three months before it was due but Jāsim al-Mutawwa' was unable to honour his liability. His brother, Najīb al-Mutawwa', also had financial problems: he had concluded a sale of shares for which he paid in five-year postdated cheques to a securities consortium. The group of senior businessmen and financiers with whom he dealt, who were also the founders and members of the board of directors of the securities consortium, presented their cheques early but the banks refused to pay, on the grounds there was insufficient credit to cover the transaction. Najīb al-Mutawwa' was declared bankrupt as a result.[4] The events set up a chain reaction as others also defaulted. August 1982 was the beginning of the end for the unregulated Al-Manakh money market.

The collapse of Al-Manakh caused a financial tremor on a scale previously unknown in the Arab Gulf Region and a major scandal both inside and outside Kuwait. A Western financial expert commented, 'The golden eagles of the Gulf have been crushed',[5] in a reference to the financial reputation of the Kuwaiti investors, thought to be amongst the most intelligent and skilful financiers and businessmen in the Arab world. Holding the Government to blame for the crash, the Kuwaiti National Assembly asked it to resign in order to restore confidence in the trading community. The Arab and world stock exchanges followed developments closely and took measures to minimise the impact of the collapse on other investments. There were also fears that Kuwait or other Gulf states might withdraw their deposits from the banks of the United States or Western Europe in order to support the local market.

Evidence of such fears is the enquiry sent by the US State Department to the US Embassy in Kuwait, to ascertain whether the Kuwaiti Government would find it necessary to draw on their foreign investments and reserves in order to finance a rescue operation.[6] The report started with a survey of Kuwait, its oil revenues and investments, the emergence of the Kuwaiti stock exchange and its unofficial parallel, Souq Al-Manakh. It explained the movements of the market and how deeply involved the individual Kuwaiti and Gulf investor had become. The questions asked by the US Department of State were as follows:

> Has the Government any choice other than to draw on the reserves of foreign assets held outside Kuwait?
> To what extent can banks honour their obligations?
> Which sector has been worst hit?
> How would the collapse of the financial market affect Kuwait's foreign aid programmes and its ability to provide security and protection from Arab extremists, such as the Palestinians or the Iraqis?

The telegram was signed by the Secretary of State George Schultz, an indication of the importance attached by Washington and the Reagan Administration to the crisis and a measure of the concern over its possible impact on US interests. The report was detailed but went out of its way to be sensational and to misrepresent some of the facts. The US Embassy failed to understand that what was happening in Kuwait in 1982 had happened before in the United States. The Wall Street Crash and the American Great Depression were amongst the world's gravest crises, lasting from 1929 to 1934.[7] The US Embassy's reply was not based on sound economic reasoning. It failed to realise that economies are cyclical and go through both active and stagnant cycles. It limited the main causes of the collapse of Al-Manakh to negligence, excessive liquidity, lack of awareness and manipulation by ministers and senior officials.

Amongst US and Western papers which published reports on the crisis, the *Washington Post* published an article on 24.11.82 under the heading, 'The Collapse of the Kuwaiti Stock Exchange of a turnover of US$ 90bn'; The *Wall Street Journal* published an investigation by Peter Trowel on 2.12.82 under the heading, 'The chickens came home to roost for all Kuwaiti dealers. The country is still rolling'. *Atlantic Monthly*, a US magazine, issued a feature on the crisis in May 1983, accompanied by the US Embassy reports. The *Financial Times* published a number of different articles, such as 'Al-Manakh crisis hits at the heart of social structure'.

Causes of the Crisis

Growth of the Market in the Absence of Institutions or Legal Framework

Chapter 3 explained the forces, both local and international, which contributed to the success of the Al-Manakh stock exchange, particularly from the middle of 1981. Several factors had coincided to push the market into a spiral of reckless and uncontrollable growth. The enormous volume of shares and wide scope of the market pushed the entire population, from officials down to junior civil servants, to trade and to invest their life savings without thought of the consequences.[8] The meteoric growth was built on foundations too fragile to sustain further development and was a direct cause of the collapse.

The Kuwaiti government failed to ensure that the law was observed, in spite of the fact that laws existed to govern both the foundation of new companies, their management structure and their regulations (Act No. 15/1960 and Act No. 3/1975, see Chapter 1). These laws safeguarded the interests of Kuwaiti shareholders and the regulation of Kuwaiti public companies. Later, when the first Gulf company was formed, the Ministry of Commerce halted all subscriptions to its shares in Kuwait and for a time, paradoxically the Ministry banned subscription to a Gulf company's shares while allowing the company to open a registered office in the country.[9] It was only later that the Ministry approved the publication of notices and balance sheets of Gulf companies in the Kuwaiti press.

The Ministry tried unsuccessfully to control the legal status of the Gulf companies whose shares were circulating in the official market, but the founders of these companies managed to evade all restriction. The Ministry of Commerce and Industry designated Al-Manakh an unofficial market by putting it beyond the reach of existing law,[10] but its officials were persuaded that non-Kuwaiti companies were not subject to Kuwait's jurisdiction. Amongst the contradictions was the sight of government officials who were issuing orders to halt dealing in the shares of such companies, rushing out to play the market themselves and to incorporate fresh ventures. Kuwaiti society was involved, from state officials down to the most humble individual.[11] The beneficiaries included brokers, founders and newcomers, subscribers and speculators. The vested interests were too deeply woven into the fabric of the country for strict measures to be put into action, especially in a state whose constitution is based on respect for personal freedom. The state therefore tacitly allowed Gulf company shares to circulate outside the official stock exchange. It was a compromise between two contradictory requirements: to protect the nation's finances; and not to obstruct a Kuwaiti who wanted to increase his wealth through speculation, however much he went against the law in doing so.

In November 1981, the Ministry of Commerce finally gave full recognition to Al-Manakh. The official blessing followed a reconciliation between Gulf company chairmen and the Minister, which convinced the government that these companies represented an important sector of the securities' markets. When the Kuwaiti Chamber of Commerce asked for Gulf companies to be given legal status, it was felt the application ought to be accepted without delay. This opinion was presented to the securities committee, which put forward conditions for acceptance. A consultative committee consisting of representatives of the companies and the Ministry of Commerce and Industry was set up to devise terms by which existing companies could be admitted to the official Kuwait stock exchange and to deal with the status of such companies during the period of transition.[13] The terms were no burden on the companies — more a sign of weakness on the part of the Ministry. The conditions included the requirement that every company should submit its annual balance sheet to the Ministry, which would monitor the information and attempt to curb the fragmentation of shares. No new company could put its shares into circulation without obtaining official approval before the announcement of the formation of the company. The committee began work at the beginning of 1982 and established a bureau through which the Ministry of Commerce could monitor and record dealings in the market and publish an official bulletin of Gulf share prices. The bureau opened on 6th March 1982, five months before the crisis. The official framework for full recognition of Gulf companies that was finally agreed permitted them to open offices for share transfers, and to participate in the market under the supervision of the Ministry's bureau and the direction of the provisional consultative committee for the Gulf companies.[14]

The reforms made the Gulf companies and Al-Manakh function more chaotically than before, but within the framework of the law. The Ministry did not redress abuse or establish order, but simply followed existing trends. The committee delegated to supervise stock exchange transactions was made up of the speculators, directors and chairmen whom it was supposed to discipline. Souq Al-Manakh had imposed itself, with all its defects and problems, on the Ministry of Commerce.[15] According to Khālid Jasīm Al-Marzūq, the Minister of Commerce and Industry, the State would limit registrations to profitable industrial companies, so as to allow their shares to be circulated. In theory, there were penalties for companies which gave false figures; the law also ruled against Kuwaiti companies that went to the market within four years — a measure designed to secure steady growth for the stock exchange. However, traders on the parallel market got round the measures by selling forward.

Here the question must be asked: once the Minister felt there was something wrong, why did he not close down the market? The market continued to lack a legal framework to control it and regulate its transactions. It had no clear traditions to follow, since a stock exchange was new to Kuwait. Ministers, members of the National Assembly, Under Secretaries of State, members of ruling families, directors of financial institutions and directors of banks all played the market and would try to block any law impinging on that market. After the crisis, the Kuwaiti daily *Al-Watan* published an article in which it criticised the ministers for their share dealings. *Al-Watan* said:

> We do not like to see ministers getting involved in share dealing. We blame the members of the National Assembly for having let such a matter pass unnoticed, the more so if it is proved that Ministers' dealings in shares affected the discharge of their ministerial duties. Some say the market crashed because the ministry spent their time hunting bargains on the stock market — leading to fears that they took advantage of public office to realise private gains. It is for such reasons that Article 131 of the Constitution expressly prohibits any person from combining a ministerial post and commercial practice.[16]

When the Minister for Commerce was asked privately whether officials had been involved in the crisis as investors, he did not deny the fact. Opting for a diplomatic reply, which implied that the report was true, he said:

> Kuwait has a small population. People were trading, buying and selling long before any emergence of the stock exchange or Souq Al-Manakh. Any loss or damage that affects the rank and file of Kuwaiti investors immediately affects government officials in view of our intertwined social relations, our affinity and parentage systems. Kuwait is one family in the sense that the interlaced social relationships have created interlaced economic relationships.

Most political grandees had share portfolios and employed their own brokers. Most Gulf companies numbered members of ruling families among their founders. Speculators who wanted to form a closed company needed only to invite a politician or a relative to join.

In a strong attack on the Government published by the magazine *Al Majalla*, the editor, al-Tajammu' al-Dinī wrote, 'It is regrettable that the person who opened the door to the practice of acting on behalf of the dealers in this market . . . the first one to break the highest value of this market, namely confidence . . . was the wife of an authority on economics.' He was referring to the lady who presented a postdated cheque.

Speculating and Forward Dealing

Investors refused to learn. The Kuwait market had suffered from dishonest practices in 1973 and 1976: imaginary subscriptions, unrecorded transactions and artificially inflated prices.[17] No sooner had Al-Manakh exhausted one cycle than investors repeated on a larger scale the same dishonest practices as before. Buyers offered forward prices as much as 300 or 500 per cent above the current price, paying by a cheque postdated three months, six months or a year later, sometimes even longer. The buyer would collect the shares immediately and dispose of them. The vendor received the cheque, and either waited until the date it fell due or transferred it to a third person from whom he had in turn bought shares. Dealers made extensive use of this device, which made it possible for speculators who had no cash in hand to pay by postdated cheque.[18] Since such cheques required no bank balance, virtually anybody was able to participate in spite of the penalty of five years' imprisonment for anyone who signed or endorsed a cheque with no bank cover at the time of signing. To encourage dealers to avoid using postdated cheques, the law allowed the cheque to be collected immediately it was presented, regardless of its date.[19] In such cases the bank was legally obliged to pay the cheque at once. In spite of this law, the signing of postdated cheques became the basis of dealing in forward buying transactions, reinforced by mutual trust between trading partners. Cheques changed hands dozens of times each day, while investors relied on the precedent that no-one would ever present a cheque before it fell due.

Postdated cheques were one of the principal causes of the escalation in share prices. It was not uncommon for prices to double within a few hours. This encouraged hectic activity in the market, in spite of the fact that some banks were unable to carry on extending facilities while others showed reluctance to offer full financing. The Central Bank imposed stringent controls and forbade banks to extend excess credit. However, the speculators no longer needed banks. Having built up their own 'futures market', they could finance their transactions with postdated cheques,[20] a new monetary structure which escaped all control.

In May 1982, about four months before the crisis, the aggregate value of postdated cheques issued amounted to KD 3,500m; together with premiums of KD 1,225m, the outstanding total was KD 4,725m. Most of the cheques were dated to the end of 1982.[21] It created an impossible situation. Numerous individuals warned of the grave consequences of letting such speculation run rampant. But the Government machines failed to stop, curb or even control the spread of forward buying. The situation led to a shortage of cash on a gigantic scale, made worse because a number of speculators had exhausted their borrowing limits both in Kuwait and in the other Gulf states. The shortage of liquidity led local companies to arrange joint loans for speculators. Investors suffering from acute cash shortages when there was none forthcoming from the banks, presented the postdated cheques they had accumulated before they fell due, which started a chain reaction: the drawers' bank accounts were overdrawn; they too presented their postdated cheques so as to bring their accounts into credit. Confidence collapsed. Prices tumbled and most people suffered enormous losses.[22] After the crash, the Kuwaiti Finance Minister 'Abd al-Latīf Al-Hamad declared that 28,800 such cheques had been recorded, with an aggregate value of over US$ 92bn. Eight dealers alone had signed cheques to the amount of US$ 63bn, and were the main cause of the collapse.[23]

During the crisis, cheques reverted to normal and once again represented cash in hand. Those paid by postdated cheque presented them for encashment. Liquidity dried up in the absence of sufficient cash, for the nominal value of mutual indebtedness was several hundred times higher than the real monies which originally constituted the transactions.[24] None of the solutions to the crisis could come to terms with the enormous sums involved and the interlaced system of relationships among the traders.

3. *Plenty of Money but no Development Plan*

Riches had flowed abundantly as a result of the oil prices moving from US$ 1 per barrel to US$ 24 in a few years, especially during the period from 1976 to 1981. Increasing money surpluses were released to a limited population and a restricted market. Had they been put to the best use, they would have transformed Kuwait into an industrial society with alternative resources and diversified its economy, but the economy was in its infancy and had no long-term development plan. Instead, the surpluses were invested in property or in bank deposits, treasury bonds or shares. Money kept producing money in a vicious circle.

Lack of Coordination Between Kuwait, UAE and Bahrain

The heart of the problem was the Gulf companies which led the market to catastrophe. The companies had dubious legal status in Kuwait, and existed free from control by the licensing authorities of the UAE and Bahrain. They operated in a country which had not granted them permission to operate but survived and grew by stealth and deceit. The UAE and Bahrain had no scruples in issuing licences without coordination with Kuwait nor amongst themselves. The government officials in the licensing countries were well aware that many such companies were no more than paper companies, formed as 'carriers' to circulate other companies' shares on Al-Manakh, and not to achieve the objectives set out in the company's Articles of Association.

Obtaining a licence was so easy that Kuwaitis rushed to acquire them, taking advantage of Kuwait's and the other Gulf States' 'free market' approach. The absence of a joint plan led the UAE and Bahrain to issue licences to non-productive companies. As part of its half-hearted attempt to control these companies and to curb the incorporation of new ones, the Ministry of Commerce in Kuwait sent an envoy to Bahrain and each of the Emirates in May 1981 to discuss a coordinated approach.[25] The attempt achieved limited results in Sharjah but otherwise failed, and the chaos of new companies persisted.

Entry of New Investors in the Market

Investors began to include people without experience, which lowered dealer confidence. Such confidence was a vital prerequisite for dealing in the market especially with postdated cheques. Many newcomers had done well on the Kuwaiti stock exchange and with property transactions before turning their attention to Al-Manakh. Their main objective was greed and the urge to seek prestige through acquiring a chairmanship or a directorship.[26]

Among the new speculators were a number who came with little to lose, people of modest origins or former civil servants, who seized an unrepeatable opportunity to improve their financial status. The majority of those involved in Al-Manakh belonged to the families of the *nouveaux riches* rather than to the traditionally wealthy families prominent in the economy and in major businesses.[27]

Lack of Advice, Guidance and Information

Mediators and brokers were not in the business of giving advice. To them, the mediator's role was just to get 1 Fils from both buyer and seller of each share negotiated (KD 1 = 1,000 Fils). Establishments which were supposed to keep detailed records did little constructive work, having only one end in view — to maximise income even if that meant supplying misleading information. The absence of any control on the activities of mediators and brokers left them free to disregard the customary practices of a stock exchange.[28] It was possible to find discrepancies in the price of shares between one broker and another. The mediator's role could be ambiguous. Moreover, the brokers who operated in Al-Manakh were deemed to be acting unlawfully because it was an unlawful securities market. The indulgence of some Kuwaiti newspapers towards share trading led them to misrepresent facts about the stock exchange and thereby mislead a large sector actual or potential traders. Such papers published false information on share prices, side by side with illogical analyses, under sensational headlines, and publicised only major transactions. An editor of one newspaper is believed to have realised about US$ 34m in profits.[29] The *Al-Seyassah* Kuwaiti daily commented in September 1982:

> Perhaps the most apt comment was one made by an economist who visited the various departments of Al-Manakh and observed the movement of people in and out of the market. His comment was that Al-Manakh had now become a centre for the distribution of wealth, whether through closed companies through which the economy had become a collective one, or through the public companies whose stock was openly available. This economist saw Al-Manakh as a centre for the accumulation and distribution of wealth, and a centre for the collective economy which was taking place within a new economic order.

Nothing could be further from the truth.

Other Factors which Precipitated the Crisis

Political and Military Developments in the Middle East. It is said that capital is a coward that thrives only in a peaceful climate and in countries which enjoy political stability and security. Only in such countries can there be economic progress, development plans and genuine investment. Whenever capital is threatened, its productive tools grind to a halt, and it leaves for more stable areas. The Arabian Gulf region is a newly developed area with a good climate for investment especially since the oil flows enriched the region since the Second World War. It is a region which has enjoyed security and political stability but of late have been troubled by relative instability and doubts over the future. The Gulf region is a small area of interlaced borders and overlapping interests. The expulsion of the Shah of Iran in 1979 and the establishment of a republican regime whose policies and tendencies were not known at the time created an atmosphere of anxiety amongst dealers and investors which seeped from the stock exchange into all sectors of the economy. However, after a while, the economic machine resumed normal functioning although the apprehension remained. In September 1980, war broke out between Iraq and Iran, 100 miles from Al-Manakh. Iran bombarded cities on Kuwait's borders and threatened to advance southwards into the Arabian Gulf States.

The outbreak of this war affected economic activity and disrupted the stock exchanges for a while. The growing anxiety halted the flow of capital into Kuwait and prompted large numbers of investors to reduce their liquidity in Kuwait and move it abroad to more stable places. However, people eventually got used to the war and business returned to normal in many ways. Nonetheless, the shadow of the unresolved conflict, which began in September 1980, affected Al-Manakh's fall nearly two years later. The destabilising effect of Israel's invasion of the Lebanon in the summer of 1982, which coincided with the months during which the market started to crack, fuelled existing fears.

High Interest Rates in the US. The economic policies of President Reagan also affected the market. Interest rates of 20 per cent and more in the US, set to attract the world's dollar funds back to the States, created a dearth of foreign currency revenues in many countries. Many transferred their liquid funds into dollar deposits, which lead to an enormous rise in the US dollar exchange rate.

Reduction in Oil Output. The reduction in oil production damaged the economic activity of the Gulf States. Less oil meant lower revenues, austerity programmes and the abolition of development projects. Gulf governments stopped pumping cash into the market and cut spending on public services and amenities. In Kuwait, dealers encouraged the general public to believe that the market would escape the cuts because it was governed by government guarantee. People had blind confidence in the state. Going on the precedent set in 1977, when the government had spent KD 155m[30] to save the market from collapse, they could not conceive that its current and accumulated oil resources would fail to constitute a foolproof guarantee against market risk this time too.

In 1977, the government had bought shares extensively and increased domestic spending in an attempt to reflate the economy,[31] but the amounts were small and the circumstances more favourable.

Auditing Firms and Falsified Reports. Accountancy firms colluded with the boards of Kuwaiti and Gulf companies to submit inaccurate reports on their financial standing. Some auditors presented false statements and balance sheets that showed profits where there weren't any. The boards paid dividends of 15 or 20 per cent by drawing from capital. One loophole in company law was that auditors were appointed at the annual general meeting for only one year. The short engagement made the accountant vulnerable to the threat of non-renewal of the appointment. The Accountants' Society had no statutory power to protect or discipline, so malpractice involving many well-known and long-established auditing firms was rampant.

Although the dangers that threatened the stock exchange gathered momentum and became intermittently obvious to some, they were disregarded by many dealers, while speculators may not even have suspected their existence. Their ignorance constituted a further problem.[32]

As the crisis hit, accusations were levelled against the government. Responsibility for the crash was laid squarely on the state by analysts and even by the legislative authority of the National Assembly represented by its elected members. The accusations were addressed directly at the government together with demands for immediate intervention to solve the crisis and to protect the reputation of Kuwait. People had become accustomed to a government which accepted heavy burdens as a result of other people's mistakes in order to support the economy. Traders had gambled on the government's intervening to buy enough shares to compensate their losses and return prices to their normal level.

When the crisis started and the market was disrupted, people were not aware of its magnitude and the serious consequences that were to follow. Some believed that it was confined to a limited number of individuals who were described by 'Abd al-'Aziz al-Saqr, the president of the Kuwaiti Chamber of Commerce and Industry, as small investors who lacked discretion and experience. In spite of the outbursts against the government, the official authorities opted to wait and see. The first step they took was to summon all major investors to Kuwait, as most were then resident outside Kuwait in their summer resorts. A private plane was sent to bring them back, and they arrived in late July 1982.[33]

The government asked them to assume their responsibilities, stating emphatically that it was not going to intervene directly. Several meetings were held between the Minister of Commerce and major speculators to find a way out of the crisis. A delegation of the dealers and market chiefs visited the Prime Minister of Kuwait, Shaikh Sa'd al-Abdullah al-Sabah, in mid-August 1982, for discussions.[34] The Government began to intervene gradually as the dimensions of the crisis became apparent. The Minister of Commerce and Industry held a press conference on 17th August at which he declared that urgent measures would be taken shortly, in collaboration with the private sector, to alleviate the situation.

A temporary ban was imposed on new private companies, with the exception of small family firms. Amongst the most important measures was one to set up an offset venture between the local banks and the public investment house, while the Kuwait Central Bank studied what credit facilities to make available to the money market.[35] Both repercussions to the crisis and counter measures were felt sooner than was anticipated, reaching the proportions of a national crisis. 'The dagger of the crisis has almost reached the arteries of Kuwait's economic structure', said the newspaper *Al-Watan*.[36] According to Ahmad 'Alī al-Du'ayj, a former chairman of the board of directors of the Kuwaiti Real Estate Investment Group, 'All are involved in the Manakh crisis. It is easy to blame eight or nine people for the crash, but the problem is that if those fall, many others will join them.'[37] The Finance Minister, 'Abd al-Latīf al-Hamad, said, 'Those who have debts must repay them or they will be sent to prison. To honour one's obligations is the only way to restore confidence. Those who kept their word have nothing to fear. I have no regrets in adopting this harsh attitude because the reputation of Kuwait can only be restored if we are strong.'[38]

The religious groups took advantage of the situation to launch direct attacks on the government.[39] Ismā'il al-Shatī, a member of the board of directors of the Reform Society and editor of *Al-Mujtama'*, the mouthpiece of the religious societies in Kuwait, wrote, 'Souq Al-Manakh is a gambling table. This market has made Kuwait live for the past five years in a state of financial psychosis. Now, the false ethics of the Kuwaiti market have collapsed. Words such as "honour", "solidarity" and "confidence" have lost their meaning. Souq Al-

Manakh has damaged the religious, social and educational life of this country. People have found it easy to do what is prohibited in a religious society, which they used to refrain from. Families have lost the leadership and guidance of their men, who were at Souq Al-Manakh.' *Al-Mujtama*'s editor accused the government of being the main culprit in the destruction of the economy: 'Its blind eye to all that was going on points to its guilt. Moreover, the government did well out of the chaos, for people were too preoccupied with Souq Al-Manakh to have any time left to bother about current political events. On the local level, the Government passed the Public Meetings Act while the people were in a coma. It almost passed its amendments to the constitution. It kept working on the notorious Article 35 of the Publications Act while the people slept. Souq Al-Manakh was a nightmare, or a dream from *The Arabian Nights*; and the morning after, people awoke to realise the grand illusions they had lived through had been no more than a dream either.'[40]

Others attributed the crash to other factors and exonerated the government. In an interview with the *Financial Times* the Speaker of Kuwait's National Assembly, Muhammad Yūsuf Al-'Adasānī, considered that what happened in Al-Manakh was an extension of the international economic crisis. The causes of the Kuwait crisis were compared to those which had thrown the world into economic crisis.[41] Shaikh Sa'ad Al Abdullah Al-Sabāh said that the market's fall had been created by particular dealers seeking quick profits, who had transgressed the rules and ethics that are a part of the trading traditions of Kuwait.[42]

Yet another group saw the crash as a positive development that should have happened earlier, because as long as the status quo continued the problem could not be dealt with. Capital had moved away from productive activity to the licensed gambling market. This made the eventual outcome inevitable, and contributed to the unfair distribution of income.[43]

As Kuwait was a rich country, it was held, it had no need to import capital or borrow from any quarter; the whole issue was just the crash of a number of major speculators on the market and the fall of a collection of paper companies — a fall which this group considered a gain for the national economy.[44]

Despite the chorus of contradictory views and proposals, the government remained cautious. Its first move was through the Ministry of Commerce and Industry. The cabinet discussed the crisis on 21st August, at its regular weekly meeting, but did not take the decision to intervene. The Minister of Commerce and Industry told a press conference on 23rd August that the government had reviewed the state of the stock market to make sure the economic situation of Kuwait was sound. The Minister described it as 'strong and intact'. But, he admitted, in view of the actions of some dealers in the stock market and their consequences, urgent steps had to be taken.

However, events were developing rapidly. Every day, postdated cheques were increasing the total debt; people were confused and Kuwait's reputation was shaken. Traders and market sharks tried to force the government into rescuing the market. Spot prices tumbled, as both Al-Manakh and the official stock exchange went downhill. The crisis had been looming since April; its first symptoms appeared in July and erupted in August. It escalated from then on in an atmosphere where everything was collapsing and falling to pieces. Everyone deluded himself that it was not his problem until the fecklessness reached the whole population and left no alternative to the government but to intervene.

The solution went through several stages and took a long time. The volume of trading amounted to KD 24bn, equivalent to US$ 92bn. The amounts drawn on by postdated cheques were astronomical. There were over 5,000 dealers representing various strata in Kuwaiti society. Their assets were not enough to cover what they owed. Many suffered heavy losses, especially among the middle income group who had gone with the rise in share prices and entered the market at its peak.[45] *Al-Watan*, the Kuwaiti daily, estimated the total value of postdated cheques to be more than three times the loans given by the IMF to the whole world in 1981, and over a quarter of the accumulated debts of third world countries (more than 100 countries) by the end of 1980. The amount was more than 17 times the official reserves of Kuwait, over 4 times those of Saudi Arabia (1980 figures), 14 times the international loans and grants made by the OPEC states in 1980, equivalent to 3½ times the official international loans and grants-in-aid made by the member states of the OECD in 1981, 1½ times the imports of each of UAE, Saudi Arabia, Kuwait and Libya during 1979, and more than the total exports of the same countries, including oil, for the same year.[46]

Kuwaiti Government's Intervention — August 1982 to end 1984

The Kuwaiti government turned to the private sector and financial institutions as they were, in the government's eyes, the parties most directly concerned. The resolution of the Council of Ministers of 21st August 1982 was based on the view that a joint initiative would be in their best interests and those of the market. The Minister of Commerce and Industry announced on behalf of the Council the formation of an offset company, through which local banks and investment companies would liaise with the Central Bank to study appropriate measures to make credit available to the stock market. The offset company was to determine debts and claims for settlement as they came and according to the dates on which the cheques fell due.[47] It was formed early in September. In another step the Consultative Committee formed by the Kuwaiti Government in early 1982 to supervise the market was asked by the Ministry to meet the major dealers.

As the offset company and its committees began work, it became clear that the market was ready to come to grips with reality at last. Dealers announced their intention to settle amicably, according to Kuwait's commercial traditions of honour, and to help the offset committees.[48]

The government set up a public company to restore regular trading within Al-Manakh, which led the way by keeping to the standards recognised in international stock exchanges. Capitalised at KD 300m, held jointly by Kuwaiti firms (51 per cent) and Gulf companies (49 per cent), the company injected liquidity into the market and set a ceiling for prices.[49]

The government put funds into the Kuwait Offset Company so that it was in a position to settle authenticated claims. It instructed the Central Bank to ease restrictions on other banks in order to provide liquidity to float investors and give dealers the necessary facilities.[50]

In the first week of September, the Kuwaiti Offset Company published a notice in the national press announcing that it had instructed the Kuwait National Bank to monitor all offset deals, both administratively and technically. The government urged the Foreign Investment Corporation and the Kuwaiti Investment Corporation, in both of which it held a major share, to secure the financial cover to conduct regular purchases of Kuwaiti shares. This was a departure from previous practice, when companies bought up as many shares as possible of companies listed officially on the Stock Exchange Rosters. The government's aim was to dislodge share prices from the high levels at which they had been frozen, and to move them gradually and regularly downwards until they reached a level at which the market could operate again.[51]

The major dealers were put under house arrest and ordered not to leave the country. The government stopped all transfers of assets from Kuwait.[52] By 5th September, the Offset Company and committees saw

✓

the first concrete results of their work, when a group of dealers announced they had settled their disputes and torn up their cheques. The ad hoc committee formed to settle the position of Jāsim Al-Mutawwa', which was considered to be the most involved, concluded its task and settled his balance the same day.[53] There were so many committees that dealers found it difficult to know where to go. The dealers' own committee wanted to settle for lower deductions, a different priority to that of the Offset Committee which was concerned with reducing the premiums on spot prices.

On 12th September, the government suspended all forward dealing. The Ministry of Commerce set up a temporary committee consisting of Jāsim al-Saqr, Salāh Ahmad Al-Ayyūb and 'Abdallah Jāsim Sdīrāwī to regulate forward dealing. The Coast Company in Ras Al-Khaimah, Sharikat al-Sāhil, was commissioned to list spot prices of Gulf shares from 1.1.81 to 9.9.82. The Committee asked all dealers to submit fresh lists of credits and debits, some of which were to be registered with the Offset Company before 1.10.82.[54] But the problems persisted and the solutions were inadequate. The Committee was caught in a vicious circle. An economic delegation set up by the merchant community met the Prime Minister of Kuwait on 13th September and delivered a memorandum putting forward three solutions:

1. Holders of cheques falling due would get their rights in full as per the cheques in their possession.
2. The value of each cheque would be paid in three instalments: 25% immediately, 25% 3 months later; the balance 6 months later.
3. Interest would not be added after payment had been rescheduled.

The proposal would satisfy the government's desire to secure maximum protection for small and medium-sized investors and to provide liquidity to cover spot obligations.[55]

However, the liability of many dealers far exceeded their shares-in-hand, whose prices were dropping sharply. The Government came to the conclusion that all measures taken thus far were unhelpful and that the protection of Kuwait's financial reputation and economic stability justified direct intervention.[56] It called a supplementary meeting on 13th September 1982, after which 'Abd al-'Aziz Husayn, Minister of State for Cabinet Affairs announced: 'The Cabinet has reviewed the circumstances of the market at the present time and in the light of consultations and recommendations, the Cabinet has resolved that a decree shall be promulgated to tackle the issues under review in such a way as to secure the continuity of dealings, guarantee fairness and restore confidence.'[57]

From 20th September the Government's direct measures began to appear. Sometimes in its own name, sometimes in collaboration with the National Assembly and the Kuwaiti Chamber of Commerce and Industry, it issued a series of resolutions and laws. Most dealt with one element of the crisis, and failed. We shall review the legislation passed from the start of the crisis until the close down of Al-Manakh in November 1984.

Acts Passed from 1982 to 1984

Act 57/1982: Forward Dealings Related to Company Shares. This Act was passed on 20.9.82 and consisted of nine Articles.[58] Article 1: all forward dealings effected prior to the coming into force of the Act were to be recorded with the Kuwaiti Offset Company within 30 days of the said decree becoming effective. Article 2: provided for the setting up of one or more Arbitration Boards for the settlement of disputes related to the transactions as described under Article 1, empowering them to take precautionary actions including freezing assets and banning of travel outside the country. Article 3: all legal procedures, civil and criminal alike, in connection with those transactions and the methods of payment, including bankruptcy declaration procedures, were to be suspended until the board had decided on them. Article 4: laid down criteria and guidelines for the board to follow in settling disputes referred to it. It ruled that the board should decide on parties' rights in accordance with precedent, an assumption of good faith, due regard to the maintenance of public order and the integrity of the national economy. The board was also given powers to decide on the method of payment, to declare artificial transactions null and void, to rescind contracts and to restore the situation to what had existed before a contract was drawn up. The board's decision was deemed final. In the event of a decision not being implemented or the amount ordered not being paid, the responsible authorities could take civil and criminal proceedings, including a declaration of bankruptcy. Article 5: empowered the board to modify an agreed forward price to the spot price at the time of contract plus a percentage to be specified by Cabinet Resolution. Article 6: allowed the parties to such transactions to reach friendly settlements among themselves provided that no third party was injured and that the board was notified of such settlements. Article 7: empowered the Minister of Justice, Law and Administration to issue a resolution to organise the work of the Arbitration Boards (see Article 2). The legislator was fully aware that the provisions were temporary by nature and dictated by the need to tackle exceptional circumstances. Therefore Article 8: the Act was to run for one year, extendable a further year by decree. Article 9: the Prime Minister and Ministers were to implement the Act, each according to his jurisdiction.

On 6.10.82 the Cabinet issued Resolution No. 46/1982.[59] It consisted of two Articles: Article 1: constitution of the Arbitration Board (Article 2 of Act No. 57). The Board was to consist of five members. President of the Board was to be a High Court Judge. Article 2: the Minister of Commerce and the Minister of Justice, Law and Administration were to implement the resolution.

The Council of Ministers, having seen the results of registration of forward dealing transactions, the amounts of money involved, and the government having declared its support for public and private finance houses and its concern to protect small investors, issued Resolution No. 49/1982 on 24.10.82, which states:[60]

1. The specification of the percentage to be allocated for legitimate profit in Article 5 of Act No. 57/1982 having been left to the Council of Ministers to decide, the Council ruled that the percentage to be added to the spot price at the time of contracting was to be the same percentage as the one agreed between the two parties at the time of contract, unless they had agreed to a lower percentage. 2. The Council also decreed that if the date shown on the postdated cheque was later than 20.9.82, the value thereof was to be reduced to the spot price plus percentage for interest, representing the balance between the price of forward buying and the spot price in the proportion of the time elapsed to 20.9.82, to be paid, in cash or by the Fund.

The following will illustrate the second paragraph. If A had sold shares to B on 1.1.82, payable by cheque postdated to 1.1.83 at interest agreed upon in addition to the spot price prevailing on that date, the new Resolution of the Council of Ministers would grant B's right to the spot price, plus interest to 20.9.82 only. The remaining three months to 1.1.83 were cancelled. The Resolution therefore reduced not only the interest but also the period.

The Resolution ruled that payment should be in cash or in bonds issued by the Fund. The Fund would reimburse, in the proportion paid by it, the creditor in all his rights *vis à vis* his debtor. There followed the legal procedures which were required to implement the previous arrangements. The Resolution specified methods of payment, separate to each category, to be made to the creditors by the Treasury, which would be acting on the decision to order the debtor to pay the debt, and on the decision by the Board of Arbitration to refer him to the Public Prosecution Authorities to enforce bankruptcy procedures.

Ministerial Resolution No. 57/1982 affected the regulation of security bonds for forward dealings in shares. It complemented and confirmed Resolution No. 49, providing further elucidation especially in relation to the categories to which the Security Fund should make payments.[61] 1. Transactions not in excess of KD 100,000 were to be paid immediately on the declaration of the award by the Arbitration Board. 2. Transactions of over KD 100,000 but not exceeding KD 250,000 were to be paid in bonds maturing 6 months from the date of the award by the Arbitration Board. 3. Transactions over KD 250,000 but not exceeding KD 500,000 were to be paid in bonds maturing 12 months from the date of the first award by the Arbitration Board. 4. Transactions of over KD 500,000 but not exceeding KD 750,000 were to be paid in bonds maturing 3 years from the date of the first award by the Arbitration Board. 5. Transactions of over KD 750,000 but not exceeding KD 1m were to be paid in bonds maturing 4½ years from the date of the first award. 6. Transactions of over KD 1m but not exceeding KD 1.5m were to be paid in bonds maturing 5½ years from the date of the first award of the Arbitration Board. 7. Transactions over KD 1.5m but not exceeding KD 2m were to be paid in bonds maturing 6 years from the date of the first award by the Arbitration Board. Within any of the classifications listed above, individual amounts might be totalled if the aggregate sum exceeded the maximum. Any excess was carried forth into the next band.

Resolution 57/1982 also ruled that no payments due to any one person should exceed KD 2m, and any applications for payments in excess of KD 2m would be disallowed. In other words, if A claimed off B the amount of KD 4m, A should have the option either to apply to the Arbitration Board and be content with KD 2m, renouncing the balance of his claims; or disclaim his right to benefit of the Security Fund, and chose to recover his money in accordance with the laws and regulations enacted by the Minister of Finance.

Pursuant to Resolution No. 57, the Minister of Finance issued Resolution No. 5/1983 to regulate what came to be known as the Fund for Security and Share Transactions. It was established at a capital of KD 500m to be paid from the State Public Reserve. The Fund was to collect 1 per cent of the basic value of any cheque, which was to be transferred to the State Public Reserve.

After the Board for Arbitration had been formed (Act 57/1982, see above), the Offset Committee established liabilities amounting to KD 26,743bn.[62] Those who were indebted for 70 per cent of the market's liabilities, or US$ 63bn, were barred by the Board from attempting to transfer or dispose of their property.[63] The eight listed names were: Muhammad Al-Ibrāhīm, Ahmad Al-Kandarī, Bāsil Al-Astā, Zayd Al-Mutawwa', Abdullah Muhammad Kabazād, the brothers Jāsim Al-Mutawwa' and Najīb al-Mutawwa'; and Hamūd Al-Jabrī, a member of the Kuwait National Assembly. They were forbidden to leave the country and their property and financial assets were confiscated under an action by the Board of Arbitration.[64] Jāsim Al-Mutawwa' was found to be the most deeply indebted of the eight men. Not yet 30, he belonged to no commercial or wealthy family. He started his career as a clerk in the passport office and then turned like many others of medium income to the stock market. He and his brother used to operate through small banking loans of only a few thousand dinars. But as a result of the market's chaos, when they operated with other people's money, they accumulated immense wealth. Their transactions were in excess of the budgets of some States, such as the Lebanon, the Sudan, Greece, Djibouti and Mauritania. Assets to the credit of Jāsim Al-Mutawwa' alone amounted to KD 6bn. After judgement, he was US$ 95m in debt.

We asked Jāsim Al-Mutawwa' about the crisis and the brothers' responsibility. Their dealing was honest, he said. Those dealers who had hurried to collect their cheques before they fell due had pushed the country to the brink of disaster. Traders used to wait for hours imploring him to conclude a transaction to purchase shares and he used to refuse. After the crisis the whole situation changed into a personal attack and he was accused of being one of the major causes. He declared he had had no intention of damaging the national economy. His sole aim had been to stimulate the money market and to stop liquidity and cash from flowing abroad.

Another of the eight debtors, National Assembly member Hamud Al-Jabrī, had settled some of his debts when his creditors dropped their rights.[65] Al-Jabrī had been in debt for approximately KD 500m, of which he repaid in cash about KD 300m before and during the crisis. He was owed about KD 150m, and remained in debt to others by KD 200m.[66]

During the recess of the National Assembly, Al-Jabrī was stripped of his parliamentary immunity in order to allow the Board of Arbitration to confiscate his property and forbid him from travelling abroad. When the National Assembly reconvened on 19th October that year, it suspended this action and issued the following statement:

> Motivated by its concern to uphold constitutional principles and the equality of all before the law, and pursuant to Article 111 of the Constitution and Articles 20 and 23 of the Regulations of the Assembly, and having seen the procedures taken against a member of that Assembly during the official recession of the Assembly and thereafter, the Assembly renounces all unconstitutional procedures taken and referred to above. It stresses emphatically that such renunciation does not mean the defence of the member but the defence of the Assembly as their legislative authority and protector of the constitution. The Assembly urges the necessity of observing duly laid constitutional procedure in respect of the removal of immunity.[67]

Act No. 57 had been passed while the National Assembly was in recess. The government therefore presented the Act to the Assembly for approval in spite of indications that the Assembly would find it difficult to pass in view of the Al Jabrī affair, which some members were likely to exploit in order to launch an attack on the government over the crisis. The National Assembly was convened on 5th October. The Emir of Kuwait, speaking for the government, promised that those who caused the crisis would be taught a severe lesson and that the rights of the people would be protected. The Prime Minister renewed these assurances during the special hearings set aside for the crisis and denied all rumours of government cover up. He stated that the government's highest priority was to save the reputation of Kuwait and the economy. It fully intended to cooperate with the Assembly in any step it might deem necessary to take within the constitutional framework. 'Abd al-Latif al-Hamad the Minister of Finance also stressed the solidity and strength of the Kuwaiti economy. He stressed that the economy of Kuwait did not derive its strength from Al-Manakh, which he described as a phenomenon that had nothing to do with the investment houses operating within and outside the country.[68]

The Minister of Commerce and Industry defended the position of his Ministry which was accused of being slow to act. He said that Al-Manakh was not an official stock exchange, and therefore was not authorised to operate. It existed within the framework of free trade, and interference would have been outside the jurisdiction of his Ministry.[69]

Some members of the Assembly disputed the constitutionality of decree 57, which had overriden their right of litigation before the judicial authority. But the Minister of Justice justified its legality by reading

Article 71 of the Constitution:

> If anything occurred in the interval between the convening of the National Assembly or at any critical interval that dictated the need to take urgent measures, the Emir had the power to issue decrees with the power of law, provided they did not contravene the Constitution or the financial estimates stipulated in the Budget law. Such decrees were to be submitted to the National Assembly within 15 days of the date of promulgation thereof if the Assembly was in session, and at the first meeting in the event of dismissal or the end of the legislative season. In the event of the Emir's failure to submit such decrees, they would retrogressively lose all power of law without any need to issue further provisions, unless the Assembly at its own discretion approved that the decrees be effective for the previous period.[70]

At the beginning of the hearing, a strong block of members voted against the decree. The government recognised that the law had certain shortcomings. The government concession made members insist on presenting an alternative. A number raised the issue of the escape to Europe of some of the major protagonists of the crisis, several of whom had obtained foreign passports.[71] 'Abd al-'Aziz Taqī had fled on an Iranian passport; Ahmad al-Muhannā on a Brazilian passport, and 'Abd al-'Aziz al-Turkī. All had kept their Kuwaiti passports, but only 'Abd al-'Aziz al-Turkī returned to Kuwait.

The deputies severely criticised the manipulators and speculators in Al-Manakh for the damage they caused to the nation's economy. A deputy, backed by nine other members including the Deputy Speaker of the National Assembly, claimed that Act No. 57 was only issued to protect major investors and ignored the small ones. The same deputy asked for the resignation of Jāsim al-Marzuq, the Minister of Commerce, charging the Ministry with being slow to move in solving the crisis which he described as having inflicted tremendous damage on Kuwait's reputation abroad.[72] After lengthy hearings, agreement was reached that representatives of the government and the National Assembly should meet within a week, from 13th October, to find a compromise formula to supplement the Act.[73]

Members of the National Assembly wished to reverse the government's compensation schemes. They maintained that the drawer of the cheque should be worried about the future and the beneficiary of the cheque should feel secure about the document he held. Decree 57 had stopped criminal and judicial procedures against those who had drawn cheques, who were now safe from litigation. It was the holder of the cheque who was left with the worry. Hence their accusation that in ratifying decree 57, the government intended to protect major investors and let down the small ones when it barred thosc who had rights from applying to the Court to secure them.[74]

Towards the end, the deputies' concentrated on specific points, the most important of which was the necessity of granting the right of litigation, the preservation of the constitutionality of any solution, the safeguarding of the full rights of citizens and the application of severer penalties to manipulators and others in the crisis. After deliberation, the law was approved together with the government's decision to set up a fund to safeguard small investors and enable them to recover their money.[75]

In retrospect, the government does not seem to have grasped the extent of the problem or its impact on the economic life of the country. New problems surfaced and got entangled with others. For instance, what about the right of citizens of other Gulf States, especially those from Bahrain and UAE, who had invested particularly heavily in Gulf companies? The traders for the citizens of the Gulf States followed closely the solutions attempted in Kuwait, where they had no power. Kuwait's government had no brief to protect Gulf investors. The most they could hope for was the cooperation of the Chamber of Commerce.

When the bearers of postdated cheques presented to Gulf States citizens went to Kuwait to register the cheques with the Offset Committee, they were told that they were excluded from any settlement since the form made for that purpose required the registration of the Identity Card Number held by Kuwaiti citizens. To all intents and purposes, this excluded from compensation all Gulf citizens and even some Arabs residing in Kuwait. The problem was that, in suspending civil and penal procedures, decree 57 had closed the Courts and all other judicial authorities to representations brought by bearers of shares.[76] The only authority empowered to register shares would not accept them, and the decree set a time limit of no more than 30 days, at the end of which if no cheques were submitted the bearer would lose all rights. Intervention by Bahrain and the UAE resolved the issue, and Kuwait decided to accept cheques issued to Gulf States citizens.

Decree 57 turned into a duel between the National Assembly and the government and deteriorated into a settling of old scores.

Act No. 59/1982: Forward Dealing and the Protection of the Rights of Debtors. This act was passed on 22.11.82, signed into law by the Emir of Kuwait, Shaikh Jabir Al-Ahmad, after approval by the National Assembly.[77] It was enacted as a result of the debate by the National Assembly on the earlier Act, on a proposal by a legislative committee formed by the Assembly for the purpose. Act 59 was the *quid pro quo* which had secured the Assembly's approval of the earlier law.

Act 59 consisted of 18 Articles, seven of which related to the regulation of the powers of the Board of Arbitration, authorising it to settle disputes without being bound to observe the rules laid down in the Civil and Commercial Procedures Act. It granted the Board the power to decide on issues of confiscation, house arrest and withdrawal of passport. The Board was also charged to refer dealers to the Public Prosecution Authorities for bankruptcy proceedings and imprisonment where it was established that they had concealed property or transferred goods abroad and failed to comply with the Board's decision to return money owed within the period specified.

Article 6 set a period of not more than two years for settlement of disputes submitted to it.

Six Articles outlined the details of a fund to guarantee debtors rights. Article 8 ruled that the Fund should be established under guarantee from the Ministry of Finance with a capital of KD 500m, to be taken from the State's Public Reserves. Article 9 outlined the objectives of the Fund, which were to secure the rights of debtors unpaid as a result of forward transactions in shares registered according to the provisions of Act No. 57/1982.

Article 10 specified the functions of the Fund as follows: (a) The repayment of debts resultant from the said transactions under paragraph 1 of the previous Article and, after delivery of the award to the creditor against the debtor and the assurance of a decision by the Arbitration Board formed under Article 1 of the said Act, to refer the debtor to the Public Prosecution Authorities for bankruptcy proceedings to be initiated against him under Article 3 of the Act. (b) To invest the monies at the disposal of the Fund in the way deemed most suitable. (c) To take all legal actions against the debtors to recover whatever payments were made on their behalf to their creditors. (d) To refund any surplus to the State Public Reserves.

Articles 14 and 15 ordered the Ministers to implement the Act, each according to his jurisdiction. Under Article 16, the government undertook to submit a full report of all the cases which were registered in time and referred to the Board of Arbitration within 30 days of the Act coming into effect and to submit a detailed report of the board's adjustments every three months.

Laws 57 and 59 both assumed that the debtor should honour his debts in full, under pain of being declared bankrupt. The Arbitration Board took on the role of debtor and paid the creditor through the Fund. The laws failed, however, to put the market and the dealers on a healthier footing. The solution to reduce the debts was rejected, which would have determined a reasonable rate of interest and kept the amount of postdated cheques within acceptable limits.

Act 57 did recognise the need for such a reduction and stressed it; Act 59 rejected the principle and stressed the universal maxim that the contract is the law of contracting parties. Article 4 of Act 57 read: 'The Board shall have discretion to lay down the mode of repayment including the payment of sums due by instalments and to declare as null and void any transactions it deems artificial or otherwise. It shall also have the power to rescind contracts and to return to the pre-contract status.'[78] Article 2 of Act 59 read: 'Without effecting any reduction in the debt unless such a reduction is reached through the Arbitration Board which may decide to settle the rights of the parties in accordance with prevailing commercial custom and the requirements of good faith in dealings while safeguarding the interests of the national economy.'[79]

The Kuwaiti Chamber of Commerce and Industry put forward its own proposals on 15th December, opening with the statement,[80] 'The Chamber has, from the outset of the crisis, striven to do its duty. But the confusion that has obscured the magnitude of the crisis had condemned to failure every endeavour to seek a solution, however hard and determined the attempt.' The Chamber's statement included the following:[81]

1. The crisis has reached such magnitude and is so entangled that it is impossible for any authority to find a solution that will satisfy all the parties or remedy the injury.

2. In spite of the Chamber's hopes that all dealers in the market would sort out this crisis with minimum injury and in such a way as not to jeopardise the financial status of any one of them, some have taken such unreasonable risks that it is not possible to salvage their financial reputation.

3. While it is internationally known that dealing in stocks and securities involves by its nature a relatively high degree of risk, transactions in the stock market of Kuwait have, according to all observers, been characterised during the previous year by a very high margin of risk verging on the brink of gambling. Therefore the Chamber believes that all traders in this market should bear a large proportion of the

responsibility for the outcome, albeit in varying degrees. Accordingly the duty to accept one's responsibilities should dictate to each trader that he not only helps his creditors but goes to the limit of what he can afford.

4. At the same time, the Chamber concedes that the conflicts of interest and the magnitude of the problem make it extremely difficult under present economic circumstances to suggest any solution without the support of the state.

5. While the first priority is to maintain a sound national economy and secure the reputation of Kuwait, there must be just punishment for anyone convicted of mishandling, manipulation or fraudulent misrepresentation.

6. Having considered many propositions, the Chamber proposes the following set of suggestions:

(a) The value of postdated cheques shall be so reduced as to halve the annual rate of interest on the cash value of the share which was the object of the transaction on the date it was concluded in relation to the rate agreed upon originally between the vendor and the purchaser, provided that such a rate shall not be less than 25% and not in excess of 50%. The amount of interest shall be calculated from the date of conclusion of the transaction to the date shown on the cheque.

(b) All cheques lodged with the Kuwait Offset Committee as a result of selling and buying of shares shall have the date on which they fall due delayed for six months, without changing the date of maturation, for which deferment the debtor who drew the cheque shall pay an annual rate of interest of 12%.

(c) The drawers of cheques lodged with the Offset Committee who have failed to sign the declaration and authorisation binding them to accept the solution suggested by the Chamber to settle debts shall not benefit from the reduction stipulated under (a) above.

(d) The Chamber suggests that the government provide funding resources through one or more instruments to be specified by the government, to facilitate the payment of dealers' liabilities.

(e) The Chamber proposes that the government shall ascertain the financial positions of the dealers and arrange for their mutual liabilities to be offset.

The Kuwait Chamber of Commerce and Industry had taken from August to December 1982 to state its position, whereas it should have been the first to speak, in its capacity as representative of commerce and traders.

The reasons cited in the preamble of the memorandum are not convincing. The memorandum is characterised by rhetoric and extreme caution.

It made only very limited attempts to tackle the problem or to reveal those who were responsible. Coming as it did in the wake of the new laws, the Chamber's memorandum is conclusive evidence that no measures, whether at state or private level, could do much to help. The very fact that the Chamber had finally proposed a solution proves the failure of those solutions already tried. The Chamber was attempting to reduce the magnitude of debts which had been left untackled by the previous laws. The Chamber also adopted the view of members of the National Assembly and some economists, that the Treasury should not carry the whole burden and that sources for funding should be sought without too much injury to the public purse.

The motion by the Chamber gained the support of dealers. Representatives of 86 per cent of the value of cheques lodged with the Kuwait Offset Committee signed the form of declaration and authorisation accepting the solution suggested by the Chamber.[82]

At the beginning of January 1983, the Offset Committee and the Board of Arbitration began work. The results of their first week's research were as follows:[83]

> Number of people who had registered with the Offset Committee: 5,509.
>
> Number of cheques submitted to the Committee: 28,878.
>
> Number of cheques for persons other than those placed under interdiction: 1,200.
>
> Number of cases of interdiction ordered by the Board of Arbitration: 60.
>
> Value of the cheques submitted to the Committee: KD 2,676,712,427,625.

On 19th January 1983, the Kuwait Offset Committee started to pay out from the Security Fund to those entitled to it on account of forward dealing, under Article 14 of the Minister of Finance's decision No. 5/1983.[84]

On 12th March, the government submitted a report to the National Assembly on the results of the working of the Arbitration Board during the period from 14.10.82–28.2.83 (pursuant to Article 16 of the Act No. 59/1982 which stipulated that the government should report every three months to the National Assembly on the work achieved by the Board).[85]

Since the law required debtors to repay in full and as contracted, bankruptcies multiplied. Nonetheless, the liquidity injected into the economy helped to set the market in motion again,[86] although it could be argued that the cash did no more than keep a dead market alive, breathing a little life into share prices.

The government presented a new draft law to the National Assembly on 16th February. At a press conference reported in the Kuwait press on 10th March, the Emir of Kuwait virtually admitted that the previous two laws had failed.[87] 'What urged us to draft the legislation under discussion now is the need to modify some of the law concerning bankruptcy', he said. 'The amendments ought, in my opinion, to help to reduce the number of those injured. We are also studying further legislation to regulate the work of the stock market, to avoid any new disasters.' The new draft was the third piece of legislation since the beginning of the crisis in August 1982.

Act No. 75/1983: Settlement of Transactions Connected with Forward Dealing. This act was passed on 20.4.83. It consisted of 25 Articles.[88] The first established an independent, judicial organisation attached to the Ministry of Finance. Its purpose was the settlement of transactions, the evaluation of the assets of those referred to it, and the administration, liquidation, control and implementation of all settlements, bankruptcies and reconciliations which come under the law. Act 75's basic objectives were:

(a) To help the creditors of the bankrupt, since the long wait while the bankruptcy assets were sorted out made it difficult for them to repay their own debts.

(b) The valuation of the financial commitments of every bankrupt before the end of the lengthy bankruptcy procedures, in order to sort out debtors and creditors.

(c) To remedy the situation created by the two previous laws, wherein the debtor of someone declared bankrupt was bound to repay his own debts promptly although unable to collect what was owing before the end of the bankruptcy procedures.

(d) To reduce cases of bankruptcy to a minimum.

(e) To entrust the supervision of bankruptcy cases to an independent neutral body, so as to avoid the properties of the bankrupt being put up for sale simultaneously.

The explanatory note to the Act stated that in order to achieve the above-mentioned objectives, the law had provided as follows:[89]

1. To found the Organisation for the Settlement of Transactions related to Forward Dealings in Company Shares.

2. To refer those whose financial position was disturbed to the

Organisation, preventing them from disposing of their goods and property, and to appoint the Organisation sequestrator (Article 4). The Organisation would prepare a report to show their real financial position (Article 5), the value of their money and size of their debts arising from forward dealings.

3. To take prompt action to define the financial situation of the debtor.

4. Friendly settlement: when the Board of Arbitration referred a person of irregular financial position to the Organisation, he would not be referred forthwith to the Bankruptcy Court but the Organisation would endeavour to arrange for a friendly settlement between him and his creditors. If such a settlement was preferred by a majority of three quarters of the creditors, it would be applied to all the creditors. Any settlement achieved in this manner would be referred to the Board of Arbitration for approval.

5. Referral to the Bankruptcy Court to be related more closely to the poor financial situation of the individual.

6. Simplification of reconciliation procedures to prevent bankruptcy. Should amicable settlement fail, the whole issue would be referred to the Court to decide whether the terms offered by the debtor in the bankruptcy prevention procedures were suitable.[90] Once the Court was convinced of the suitability of such terms, it would issue an order to that effect which would be binding on all and the debtor would no longer undergo bankruptcy procedures.

7. Offsetting of debts would take place in spite of bankruptcy (Article 17).

8. Simplification of the procedures for judicial reconciliation, and reconciliation with the disclaimer to properties. These two reconciliations would take place pursuant to an order by the Court subject to the consent of the Organisation, provided that the debtor was deemed solvent once his assets were equal to his debts.

9. All verdicts would be final. If a debt arising from forward dealings in shares was disputed, due jurisdiction to decide on such a dispute would be the prerogative of the Board of Arbitration rather than the Bankruptcy Court, which should refer such a dispute to the Board of Arbitration for an award thereon.

10. The actual value of bonds would be determined once repayments were completed, whether through settlement, reconciliation or bankruptcy. Such bonds were liable to discount or mortgage.[91]

On 17th April 1983, the Council of Ministers issued Resolution No. 16/1983 in respect of the formation of the Board of Directors for the Organisation for the Settlement of Transactions Related to Forward

Dealings in Company Shares.[92] The Board of Directors for the Organisation would be chaired by the Minister of Finance and would include the following members (Article 1):

1. A representative of the Ministry of Finance to be nominated by the Minister.
2. A representative of the Ministry of Commerce and Industry to be nominated by the Minister.
3. A judge to be nominated by the Judicial Council.
4. A representative of the Real Estate Registration Department to be nominated by the Minister of Justice.
5. A representative of the Kuwait Chamber of Commerce and Industry to be nominated by its Board of Directors.
6. A representative of the Offset Committee to be appointed by its Board of Directors.
7. Three experts and competent members to be nominated by the Council of Ministers for a period of two years, (renewable).

On 23rd May 1983, the Council of Ministers issued Resolution No. 14/21, for the year 1983, in respect of the Organisation for the Settlement of Transactions Related to Forward Dealings in Company Shares, which specified the Organisation's procedural and internal administrative rules.[93] The Prime Minister, Sheikh Sa'ad Al-Abdullah, said, after the law had gone through the National Assembly, that he thought this law would solve 80 per cent of the crisis which was then eight months old. He was optimistic, he said, that the market would resume its activity and vitality.[94]

In reality though, only 5 per cent of the problem had been solved. Hence the Government had to issue further laws bringing in new solutions.[95] Salāh Al-Fahd, the Chairman of the Board of Arbitration, summarised the situation at the time of the promulgation of this law in an interview with the Kuwait News Agency on 4th April. He said that:

> Up to the end of March the Board of Arbitration had referred 55 persons to the Public Prosecution Authorities.
>
> The Board had issued 6,328 orders in respect of the debts of these people, of a value in excess of KD 2,589m.
>
> The Board had approved 1,670 settlements between parties, for over KD 1,532m.
>
> The Board had adjudicated in more than 240 disputes.

On the surface a degree of relief was evident to some of the dealers. People not aware of the magnitude of the problem said the crisis was over, an expectation shared by those looking forward to the resumption of market activity. But in spite of all measures, the market continued to collapse. Bankruptcies were still on the increase and share certificates virtually worthless. Efforts to deal with the crisis had been shortsighted and inadequate, concentrating on the symptoms rather than the causes. The Government put KD 500m into the Security Fund and the purchase of stocks on the Kuwaiti stock exchange, but the remedy was superficial, and few benefited. The government kept issuing resolutions and media declarations to which the market thermometer usually responded with a flurry of activity.

When Kuwait's Minister of Finance talked to the *Wakh* (the Kuwaiti News Agency) on 17th March about the causes of the country's recession, he pointed firmly to the Al-Manakh crisis as the basic cause. The Minister listed four factors that influenced Kuwait's economy: the Iran-Iraq War, the world oil glut, the world economic recession which had set in for 10 years; and, at home, the people's lack of interest in the economic situation because they preferred to direct their enthusiasm to the activities of Al-Manakh. The Minister exonerated the government from responsibility for the crisis. The Kuwaiti government had realised the causes, he said, and had them under constant review but its voice was ignored since all the news concentrated on what was happening in Al-Manakh. It was only when this news fizzled out that people began to realise the general state of Kuwait's economy.[96]

From the beginning of the crisis until 1984, the government devoted all its energy to the market, devising first one solution then another. Some ministries came to a halt and the government neglected its basic duties. Even the National Assembly no longer raised its voice to comment on Arab and world events. Commenting on this, the Minister of Finance said, 'The time and effort we devoted to solving the problem made us ignore everything else.'[97]

An official said that the country had been hijacked by the crisis, run without will or general purpose. Another official said. 'I wish I could find another body to perform the basic functions of the Cabinet, leaving the present Cabinet to deal with the stock market.'[98]

Having realised that their laws increased bankruptcies, and aggravated the problems, the government decided there was an urgent need to abrogate or amend some of their provisions. If they remained in force, it was foreseen that the following would happen:[99] 1,200 more people would become insolvent. A further 128 cases would be referred to the Organisation. There would be a further increase in the number of cases before the courts and the number of bankruptcies. The

Fund would have to bleed the State Public Reserves. Dangerous negative effects would be felt by banks and institutions with a cumulative turnover estimated at KD 1,700m.

Everything that could be calculated had been analysed: size of debts, number of victims, bankruptcies and postdated cheques. The Offset Committee had been set up, the Security Fund, the Board of Arbitration and the Organisation for the Settlement of Transactions and the promulgation of several legislative instruments (Act Nos. 57/1982 and 75/1983). Still 95 per cent of the problem remained unresolved.

Many feared the collapse of the banking houses, which constituted the backbone of the monetary and financial system and with which the financial interests of the majority of people were closely linked. The Kuwaiti banking system, which in previous years had played a vital role in supporting and reinforcing the money base, had been the envy of many world monetary and financial circles. Its essential stability had allowed it to expand at local, regional and global levels. After the collapse of Al-Manakh, all the banks, and especially the Kuwaiti National Bank, suffered. Bankruptcies aggravated the problem, while the sharp slide in the value of shares and property left the banks without reliable securities against their loans. If the banks called in these securities shares would flood the market and prices tumble even further. The property market was virtually dead.[100]

Moreover, as a result of the crisis, investors began to move away from local investment instruments, such as Kuwaiti Dinar Bonds, in favour of overseas investment, where interest rates were high.

In spite of this, the integrity of the banking system was in no danger. Reserves and supplies were adequate. The Government put at the disposal of the Central Bank several devices to help the commercial banks maintain their liquidity. The devices included discount operations, whereby commercial promissory notes maturing within a year could be cashed at special interest rates; and swapping facilities with local banks, which involved the exchange of local for foreign currencies for periods ranging from one week to three months. The Central Bank was empowered to issue bonds in periods of one week, one month or three months. Those bonds would provide the commercial banks with instruments bearing interest, which could replace current account balances with the Central Bank itself.[101] However, economic crises inevitably cast doubts on the integrity of the banking system. As the Al-Manakh crisis broke, doubts were reflected in the drying up of liquidity and a sharp and rapid rise in interest rates. When the Ministry of Finance and the Central Bank both announced they were standing by the banks, the declaration helped to restore confidence.

Other economic activities were not immune from the crisis. Some were nearly paralysed. Political and military conditions made matters worse. The government realised that the three laws it had enacted had achieved very little and appealed for the cooperation of the Kuwaiti Chamber of Commerce. The Cabinet Economic Committee held a joint meeting on 27th June 1983 with the Finance Committee of the Chamber of Commerce, which submitted a report calling for a halt to further declarations of bankruptcy; and the Board of Arbitration was to be granted the power to reduce the indebtedness of bankrupts to one another and to third parties.[102] Had the government accepted these proposals, it would have been steering an unlawful course. Moreover, creditors of bankrupts would have suffered an injustice, in that they would have incurred a part of their debtors' insolvency. The injustice would have been flagrant, because dozens of other creditors had received what they were owed in full through the Fund. A double standard would have been created between those who had recovered their monies in full and those asked to make sacrifices. After lengthy deliberations, the government enacted its final measure.

Act No. 100/1983: Some Provisions Connected with the Settlement of Transactions Related to Forward Dealing. This law was passed on 14.8.83 with the approval of the National Assembly. It was over a year since the start of the crisis, and three other laws had failed to control its spread.

The new law differed essentially from the previous ones in that it was the first to adopt the principle of reducing debts. Many had advocated such an approach since the crisis started, in view of the volume of debt resulting from exaggerated premiums added to the spot prices. The government argued that the method would have the following results:[103]

A solution to 60–70 per cent of the problem, debts reduced to 40 per cent.

Seven people still in possession of a surplus of KD 40,000 would become insolvent; and a further two with a surplus of KD 730,00 between them.

Eighty-one people would move from deficit to surplus.

The number with a deficit would be reduced to 548, amounting to a total of KD 1,600m.

When this Act was presented to the National Assembly it provoked heated debate. One deputy said that the government listened only to people with a vested interest, and that the major dealers were controlling the Government.[104] Nevertheless, the government was confident of National Assembly approval, particulatly as a number of its members were themselves involved in the crisis, and could be relied on to approve anything it proposed.

This new law consisted of ten Articles and included a number of radical provisions.[105]

Article 1: under the law, all debts arising from forward dealings in shares would fall due as from the date on which the new law took effect, if they had not fallen due already. It was difficult to disentangle the mess without such a provision. The new law avoided the shortcomings of the law No. 75/1983, which set the end of 1983 as the date when all such debts would fall due. While the previous laws ruled that the debtor should repay his debts without modification, the new one decreed that debts should be reduced to the spot price on the day of the dealing, plus a percentage of profit to represent the difference between the forward purchase price agreed upon and the spot price, taking into account the time that had lapsed until the date of maturation, provided that such a percentage should not exceed 25 per cent per annum of the spot price.

The new law granted the Board of Arbitration the power to reduce the percentage to 25 per cent or even to abolish it should circumstances warrant. The Board should use its powers after reviewing the position of the debtor. Should it be revealed that the debtor had supplied false information, or made fraudulent misrepresentations, or concealed property, or disposed of it to the detriment of his creditors, or fled abroad, the law empowered the Board to restore the maximum percentage. The new law departed from the earlier ones in that it could enforce penal sanctions.

Article 2: stipulated that Offset should prevail as a rule between all dealers if the person entitled thereto insisted upon it. This should be subject to the careful observance that the debts should be reduced in the proportion of the expected deficit in the debtor's properties as assessed by the Organisation for the settlement of Forward Transactions related to the companies' shares. This was a similar provision to that of Article 2 of Act No. 59/1982.

Article 3: all awards and amicable settlements approved by the Board of Arbitration prior to the new law should stand. As for the debts due on those who were referred to the Organisation prior to the new law taking effect, if the debts had already been repaid by the Fund, the provision in respect of the reduction of the amount of debt should apply. Notwithstanding this rule, in order to safeguard the welfare of the small investors to whom the Fund had paid their dues before this law came into force, the Article provided that should the sums actually paid to them be in excess of the amount of the debt after reduction, the Fund should pay the difference, thereby serving the interests of both creditor and debtor. There was no conflict between this Article and Article 5 of the same law, which ruled that the Board of Arbitration should reconsider the awards delivered prior to the new law coming into force in the case of those dealers who were referred to the Organisation, or whose properties were attached, or who were forbidden to dispose thereof, in view of their positions calculated under the earlier laws pursuant to which the debts were payable in full. With the promulgation of the new law which provided that debts should be reduced, new financial positions were created for these dealers which should be reviewed in terms of viability or insolvency. Should the Board decide to confirm its resolution of referral to the Organisation for the Settlement of Forward Transactions, the time limit for making amicable settlements should come into force (Article 8 of Act No. 75/1983) as from the date of the Board's decision. The proposed legislation brought in a new provision to modify the time limit from three to six months, to apply to anyone referred to the Organisation.[106]

Starting from the principle of honouring equality among all creditors, paragraph 2 of Article 5 introduced a provision dictated by the General Rules, which imposed a stay of execution on all civil and commercial orders and court decisions delivered in matters other than the forward dealings in shares. Those referred to the Organisation after the new law took effect took precedence. The cases were to be decided upon according to the provisions of Act No. 75/1983, under which all creditors recovered their rights on an equal footing.

Article 6: allowed the Board of Arbitration to form sub-committees to be chaired by one of its members and to include one or more of its other members and specialist experts whom it might select from a roster to be issued by a resolution from the Minister of Justice. The sub-committees would help with preparation of cases, the compilation of necessary documents and the submission of reports to the Board in the light of which the Board would issue its award or decisions related to the relevant case.

The new law faced opposition from both National Assembly and dealers. The main objections were as follows:[107]

1. Since it was the big dealers who were solely or mostly to benefit

from the new law, it would be detrimental to the financial security of the country to place the burden of the payment of differences on the Fund, especially as the Fund's resources were taken from the General National Reserves.

2. It would solve nothing. It would merely transfer the deficit from the big investors to the small.

3. It ignored those who had paid their debts in full, who would now receive less than their dues.

4. It banned commercial legal actions before the courts.

5. Because the position of the finance houses and especially the banks was sound, there was no need to protect them from the current crisis. They had proved themselves capable of safeguarding their positions despite deteriorating conditions for the dealers on Al-Manakh.

6. Surpluses should be diverted to the creditors.

7. The manipulators who caused the crisis should be brought to justice.

Loopholes in the new law stirred controversy among dealers. One problem was that lists of spot prices for Gulf shares were not published every day during the two years 1981–82. If they had been, they would have constituted the basis of any settlement, since the new law stipulated the return to the spot price, plus interest not in excess of 25 per cent per annum on the said price. The Board of Arbitration tried to reach a compromise despite conflicting records.

Other weaknesses emerged. One was the hurried calculation of the cash possessed by the bankrupts with whom most of the dealers had made their transactions. The dealers were refusing to repay their debts in accordance with the law until they were certain about what had happened to the money owed to them by the remaining 128 bankrupts. A hurried declaration of the financial position of the debtors was reached, since the latest law made only one imperative restriction, namely a ceiling for interest that should not be exceeded. Apart from that, the new law left matters open. This created a fertile climate for adventurism and procrastination, in which the dealers tried to show a deficit and to repay at an interest rate below the set ceiling. On their part, the creditors tried their utmost to secure interest at the top rate.[108]

The Chairman of the Board of Arbitration made it clear that the Board would not reduce the interest rate below 25 per cent unless the debtor, certified by an officially audited balance sheet, was unable to meet his liabilities if interest was charged at 25 per cent.[109]

The new Minister of Finance issued regulations to ensure the law was carried out. The earlier Minister of Finance, 'Abd al-Latīf al-Hamad, whose policy conflicted with the intentions of the government, had resigned. His priority had been to curb inflation through a squeeze on public spending, but the beneficiaries from such a tense economic climate fought hard against the Minister's plans and forced him to resign. Asked about that when he was delivering a lecture at Coventry, England, al-Hamad answered that he had held a clear view about the necessity of sustaining the economic relationship between individuals, but the government had found a different course and followed it.[110]

The finance portfolio was given to Shaikh Khalīfa Al-Sabāh, in addition to the oil portfolio.

The following examples illustrate the impact of the new law on the financial positions of dealers. Some dealers had seen a deficit turn into a surplus as a result of the new law. Others, who had enjoyed a surplus, saw it turned into a deficit.[111]

A Dealer whose Incoming Postdated cheques amounted to less than his Outgoing Postdated cheques and who was in Deficit Prior to Act No. 100/1983.

Financial Position of Dealer A before application of Act 100 (KD m)

Assets		Liabilities	
10,000	Shares	40,000	Debit notes
5,000	Property	5,000	Loans
30,000	Credit notes (for shares sales)	5,000	Other debits
2,000	Other assets		
3,000	Excess of liabilities over assets (deficit)	50,000	
50,000			

On application of Act 100 (assuming the two components of the interest and periods are proportionate)

	Calculated credit notes	Calculated debit notes
Spot price	15,000	20,000
Rate of interest at 25 per cent p.a.	3,750	5,000
Value	18,750	25,000

Financial Position of Dealer A after application of the Act (KD m)

Assets		Liabilities	
10,000	Shares	25,000	Debit notes
5,000	Property	5,000	Loans
18,750	Credit notes (for share sales)	5,000	Other debits
2,000	Other assets	750	Excess of assets over liabilities (surplus)
35,750		35,750	

Dealer A realised a surplus after the application of Act No. 100/1983 because, in terms of postdated cheques, his debit side was higher than his credit.

A Dealer whose Incoming Postdated cheques amounted to more than his Outgoing Postdated cheques and who was in Credit Prior to Act No. 100/1983

Financial Position of Dealer B before the application of the Act (KD m)

Assets		Liabilities	
5,000	Shares	15,000	Debit notes
5,000	Property	5,000	Loans
30,000	Credit notes	17,000	Other
		3,000	Excess of assets over liabilities (surplus)
40,000		40,000	

The calculation of credit and debit notes after application of the Act

	Calculated credit notes	Calculated debit notes
Spot price	18,000	9,000
Rate of interest at 25 per cent p.a.	2,250	1,125
Value	20,250	10,125

Financial Position of Dealer B after application of the Act (KD m)

Assets		Liabilities	
5,000	Shares	10,125	Debit notes
5,000	Property	5,000	Loans
20,250	Credit notes	17,000	Other liabilities
1,875	Excess of liabilities over assets (deficit)	32,125	
32,125			

Dealer B suffered a deficit after he had enjoyed a surplus because his credit side in terms of postdated cheques was higher than his debit side.

The law attracted strong opposition because it favoured the big investors who had more postdated cheques to their debit than to their credit. It was the small dealers who suffered because it was they who had more postdated cheques to their credit than to their debit. The new law thus defeated its purpose, which was originally aimed at protecting the small investors.

However, the Board continued to function. In late October 1983, it decided to form a number of sub-committees to investigate and determine the positions of those referred in order to alleviate pressure on the Board and make easier the task of the auditors, whose numbers increased enormously. With Act No. 100/1983 in force powerful obstacles emerged. A shock wave hit the dealers when the value of the bankrupts' dinars was announced, at an average of .250 per dinar, because those who had debts owed by the bankrupts would receive only a quarter of every dinar to which they were entitled. At the same time they had to pay their own debtors in full. The announcement of the reduced value of the bankrupts' dinar provoked an outburst among a vast group of dealers, especially amongst those who had repaid their debts in full under the old law. Having complied with their obligation in full, the repayment of what they were owed from non-bankrupts came to 25 per cent on top of their own capital; for bankrupts, the amount was lower because a declared bankrupts' dinar was valued at less.[112] The bankrupts were those who had been referred to the Board of Arbitration and, being unable to repay their debts, had been declared bankrupt. The Board had then sequestrated and evaluated all their assets. After their debts had been calculated, assets and liabilities were weighed. If they were equal, the creditor received his dinar in full. If the assets were half the liabilities, he received 500 fils, and so on. The person who had not been declared bankrupt would pay his dinars in full plus 25 per cent in interest. Many more people were pushed into bankruptcy.

When it was found that Shaikh Khalīfa Al-Abdullah Al-Sabāh's assets did not cover his liabilities, some tried to conclude an amicable settlement in order to prevent his referral to the Board and the declaration of his bankruptcy. But others wondered if there was a double standard, where people of influence were not subject to the same law as the rank and file.[113] Khalīfa Al-Abdullah Al-Sabāh was one of the major dealers, whose liquidity amounted to KD 7bn. Any reduction of his debts would bring down many others in a chain reaction, since the others would not be able to repay any of their debts unless they received the debts owed to them. Proposals were made to reach a settlement on the basis of the payment of 25 per cent of the capital forthwith, 50 per cent six months later: the balance of 25 per cent would depend on what was left of Shaikh Khalīfa Al-Abdulla's property and assets. It was unclear whether the balance of the capital would be in excess of the 25 per cent; or whether it would be less than 25 per cent; or, most likely, whether any assets be left after payment of 75 per cent of the capital.[114] The creditors refused settlement. Bankruptcies followed one another after that in a chain reaction. The creditors of any one declared bankrupt received only a quarter of their dues; unable to repay their own debts, they too became bankrupt.

As more negative effects surfaced, many became convinced that Act No. 100/1983 was no solution and would meet the same fate as the three earlier Acts. In mid-October 1983, five members of the National Assembly submitted a proposal to found a large bank, a 'jumbo bank', with a capital of KD 3bn to help break the deadlock. The proposition was that the bank's capital would consist of the assets of the bankrupts and major dealers and would issue shares to that value. The government would contribute KD 5bn, another KD 5bn would come from Kuwaiti banks and concerns; the rest would be offered to the public for subscription.[115]

The project never saw the light of day. It met with formidable opposition from the traditional merchants and conservative economists in Kuwait. They objected that such a bank would provide fertile ground for bankrupts to speculate on its shares, and in inflating their prices, find themselves a way out of one problem only to get into another. Moreover, to set up a Jumbo Bank, capitalised in excess of the three major American banks put together, Citibank, Bank of America and Chase Manhattan, at the prevailing exchange rate of KD 3bn to US$

11bn,[116] would have created a climate of unfair competition for the commercial banks operating in the local market.

All solutions aimed to get rid of the debts and save the dealers. The market remained static. On 14th August 1983, the government issued a Decree on the Regulation of the Kuwait Stock Exchange. The Decree consisted of 18 Articles mostly dealing with stock exchange regulation, development and powers.[117]

Article 1: the Kuwait Stock Exchange should be a separate juridic entity with the legal capacity to dispose of and administer funds according to the processes of law.

Article 3: the aims of the Stock Exchange were: (a) to work towards the development of the money market in such a way as to benefit the economic development process and to contribute to the realisation and achievement of the goals set by the state's economic policies; the development and rationalisation of the methods of dealing adopted at the market in a manner best able to secure the transactions' safety, accuracy and accessibility, and to provide protection for the dealers; (b) to establish connections and contacts with foreign money markets with a view to learning the methods of dealing followed by such markets, and to make use of such information to accelerate the development of the Kuwaiti financial market.

Article 5: a Market Management Committee was to consist of the following persons: the Minister of Commerce and Industry, chairman; the market manager, vice-chairman and full-time director; a member to represent the Ministry of Commerce and Industry; a member to represent the Ministry of Finance; a member to represent the Central Bank of Kuwait; two members of proven experience and qualifications to be appointed by the Council of Ministers on the recommendation of the Minister of Commerce and Industry; and four members to be appointed by the Kuwait Chamber of Commerce and Industry, one of whose number was to be a mediator.

Article 8: specified the technical tools necessary for the conduct of the market: a prices monitor; a forward dealings monitor, whose task was to evaluate forward dealings, and the relationships between such transactions and spot dealings; and a third monitor to compile, analyse and publish information related to the market and the securities in circulation.

Article 10: membership of the market would be open to the following: Kuwaiti companies whose shares were launched for subscription by the public; those closed Kuwaiti companies which the Market Committee decided to accept; and stock mediators working on the market. The market regulations would register the mediators and their assistants, organise their activities and control their dealings.

The remaining articles of the Decree on the Regulation of the Stock Exchange dealt with the market budget and revenues, Arbitration Committees and the Committee for the Settlement of Disputes.

The Decree committed the old error of allowing Al-Manakh to grow parasitically outside the law, on the pretext that it was not Kuwaiti. Article 10 laid down rules for membership which was to consist solely of Kuwaiti companies, forgetting that the official Kuwaiti Stock Exchange was not the cause of the basic problem which had in fact been caused by the parallel market. Where then was the remedy introduced by the new decree? Where did the Gulf companies stand? When would the government take notice and acknowledge real life? It was living through a major crisis whose causes were known, and now under the new law it ignored them, unless it was its intention to kick out of the country all companies that were not one hundred per cent Kuwaiti. It was a paradox that the government had compiled enormous portfolios of Gulf shares to save these companies from liquidation. It had extended official recognition to them in one place and denied it in another.

Al-Watan wrote on its economic page on 1st September 1983 that the tattered new legislation failed to take into account the earthquake which had shaken the country and almost demolished its institutions. It had made no attempt to investigate the causes which had led to it. Another question concerned the presence of the Minister of Commerce and Industry on the Market Committee. Why should the Minister, who was a politician, preside over a permanent committee whose formation was purely technical and which had no ministerial accountability? This committee should not have had a minister as chairman. It should have been headed by an experienced full-time officer. Further, why should ministers be given the right to nominate an officer to represent them on the committee and why should the Chamber of Commerce and Industry be asked to nominate some of its members to represent the private sector? It was the private sector, which had traded the shares, which was the one that needed monitoring. How could the adversary be asked to be judge?[118]

The legislation never got off the statute book because the market had too many other worries. The government took market and dealers by surprise early in November 1983 when, without any prior notice, it stopped buying shares. The stoppage put an end to dealings and deprived the market of the liquidity injected into it through the government's daily purchases. Dealers thought that the government had lost interest in continuing to support the market. The market finally came to a complete halt at the same time as endeavours to solve the crisis ceased because the government was preoccupied with riots elsewhere. In January 1984, the government focused its attention on the market again when the Minister of Finance, Shaikh Al Khalīfa Al Sabāh, announced the scheme for Offset Arrangements, the biggest of all the plans in the history of the market's crisis.

Scheme for Offset Arrangements

This scheme comprised the following provisions: the Kuwaiti Corporation for Trade, Contracting and Foreign Investments would, jointly with the Offset Corporation, conduct offset arrangements and would use government funds to repay debts on behalf of both inter-related dealers and those referred to the Committee.

The activities of the two corporations would be subject to the supervision of a 'shadow board' which would consist of the chairman of Bargan Bank, the director general of the Kuwaiti House of Finance, the deputy chairman and managing director of the Kuwaiti Corporation for Trade, Contracting and Foreign Investments, the director general of the Kuwaiti Offset Corporation and a member of the Kuwaiti Bureau of Auditors. The Committee was to consider cases of insolvency that were still outside the jurisdiction of the Corporation. It would have the power to give instructions to the two corporations to repay the debts of someone declared insolvent, according to his means. The two corporations would act in his name to collect moneys owing to him from those referred to the Board or any others. The instructions would be issued by order of the body's Five-Man Committee and with prior coordination with the Board of Arbitration whose instructions would also be followed in respect of payment in instalments or the use of shares in part settlement.[119]

The following illustrates how the system was intended to work: suppose, for example, that the Board of Arbitration ordered a debtor to repay his debt part in cash and part in shares. The two corporations would effect the repayment on his behalf and would take his place in the settlement of any relationship he had with his creditors. If the debtor did not own any shares, the Kuwaiti Corporation for Trade, Contracting and Foreign Investments would sell an amount of shares as ordered by the Board of Arbitration and use the returns in part payment of the debt. Such an insertion of shares in the Offset arrangements by order of the Board of Arbitration would have two advantages: the first was the use of shares to absorb part of the cash indebtedness, which decreased the total volume of money; and the second was that the Corporation for Trade, Contracting and Foreign Investments, which had been one of the most prominent government mediators purchasing the shares of Kuwaiti corporations on the stock exchange for over a year, would bring back into circulation a substantial number of the shares, by returning them to the creditors.[120]

The submission of the Offset scheme was intended to push the crisis along the road to a final solution, to ease dealings between entangled dealers through government funds and to use shares to absorb part of the crisis. A power of attorney was prepared for willing dealers to sign, which authorised the two corporations to pay on their behalf.

The Minister of Oil and Finance assured a group of dealers on 8th January 1984 that there were going to be no further laws. The dealers had to choose between Offset or being referred to the Organisation for the Settlement of Transactions.[121]

The scheme met with mixed reactions. Some welcomed it because they wanted to feel that the government had not abandoned all attempts at a solution. A number of big dealers described it as an outstanding step that would help to solve the problem but regretted that it arrived at least six months too late. During those six months, many had repaid their debts in cash, and forfeited their new right to the immediate collection of their dues. They had also missed a wider choice of means of repayment including the new share element. Another group of dealers pointed out that the latest scheme missed a point of great significance, which was the completion of a correct and final evaluation of the assets of the people referred and the declaration of the ultimate value of the dinar which should be assigned to the authors of the scheme.[122]

During that period, Kuwait's economic slump hit most sectors. The Kuwait Chamber of Commerce and Industry submitted a comprehensive memorandum on the economic situation to the Prime Minister, including several demands by the Chamber, and suggested methods of reactivating the economy. The memo dealt with the four major sectors of construction, industry, trade and transport, and finance and investment.[123]

Bankruptcies continued and prices fell. Daily newspapers were regulated published advertisements from the Organisation for the Settlement of Transactions announcing the assets and liabilities of the latest bankruptcy.[124]

On 29th April 1984, the Prime Minister held a meeting attended by a number of ministers and top people in the sectors of finance and investment and the Chamber of Commerce.[125] They discussed how to stimulate the finance and property markets and agreed on suggestions to be submitted to the Council of Ministers. At a session held on 30th

April, the Council of Ministers approved measures to terminate the complications which had arisen among the dealers referred to the Organisation. The original value of debts among the referred dealers amounted to some KD 9bn. After settlements and offsets under Act No. 100/1983, and following the bilateral, trilateral and quadrilateral offset arrangements, the sum had been reduced to KD 200m and was expected to drop further.[126] It was decided to create a fund to purchase shares in order to prevent speculation on prices, another fund to insure property at high rates and on easy terms, and a third to pledge the shares of closed and Gulf companies.

The three basic funds were approved by the Council of Ministers and set to work forthwith. The First Fund was for the purchase of the property of the referred dealers for the sum of KD 840m at prices fixed by the Financing House, the Property Bank and a specialised committee consisting of three authoritative members of the market. The Second Fund began work the next day to pledge or buy property shares on behalf of the insolvent, to ensure they repaid within a year and a half.[127]

Among the early signs that the crisis was on its way to a final solution was that the affairs of the big dealers were becoming disentangled from one another, although this in itself led to new problems because of the impact of the reduction of debts on the creditors.

The greatest single problem was Shaikh Khalīfa Al-Abdullah, who had proposed to pay 75 per cent and promised to consider the balance of 25 per cent in the light of any money left. Then it was found that his assets would cover no more than 70 per cent. On 2nd September 1984, the deadlock was broken following the decision that he was to pay 70 per cent of the capital, but in hard cash. That, on its own, improved his debtors' ability to repay their debts to the local bank — such settlements would lead to others, which would ultimately lead to a solution.[128] The majority of creditors agreed only under duress, as their losses were enormous. Some considered the solution contravened the provisions of the newly promulgated Acts and suggested that because that dealer, Shaikh Khalīfa, was a member of the Ruler's family,[129] he had not been referred to the Organisation. Why should some be referred to the Organisation to be declared bankrupt and banned from travelling abroad, while judgement on others was suspended? There was comment in the papers. In a leader on 3rd September, *Al Anba'* said that the members of the National Assembly who had voted for Act No. 100/1983 should ask themselves what had happened to their intentions. 'If issuing a law does not mean its universal application,' the paper said, 'Where does that leave the law?'

Besides Shaikh Khalīfa, there were about 50 people, likely to rise to 100, who had not been referred to the bankruptcy court in deference to their social and trading status.

Dealers believed that the only workable solution was for the government to intervene, to take over all the property and shares owned by those entangled with Shaikh Khalīfa and other big dealers, and to pay the former's debts in full. They argued that the Government had already spent US$ 2,500m to support the market. However, a senior official replied, 'We cannot buy the whole country. We have acquired a great deal of the Stock Exchange and any further purchases of property will require the spending of many more billions.'[130]

Government spokesmen justified saving the big dealers from the bankruptcy court on various grounds: one was that their assets did not cover the necessary 70 per cent and that this was in particular the case with Shaikh Khalīfa Al-Sabāh. Another was that trade would suffer if such major figures were referred for bankruptcy proceedings. Moreover, they had obligations towards both local banks and international banks. Any such action against them would cause enormous damage to Kuwait's reputation as a financial centre.[131]

By the end of October 1984, several signs heralded the end of the crisis. Bonds to the benefit of the creditors appeared and their values were collected. Big creditors had been repaying their debts. Disentanglement between big dealers moved towards completion. The country started to enjoy higher liquidity, and a new stock exchange was opened.

Inauguration of the New Stock Exchange and Abolition of Souq Al-Manakh

Under the Decree issued on 14.8.83 concerning the organisation of the stock exchange, and the Executive Regulation to the Decree issued under Ministerial Order No. 35/1983, the official Kuwaiti stock exchange was moved from its old premises to a new tower building costing US$ 62m. It was formally inaugurated on 29th September 1984. The building was so vast that the Hall was considerably larger than that of the London stock exchange. The computer systems cost over US$ 10m.[132]

Khālid Al-Khurāfī, director general of the Kuwait stock exchange, declared that business would close down at the old stock exchange on Saturday 29th September. At a press conference held the week before, on the 22nd, he declared that no operation would ever again be permitted outside the new stock exchange hall under any circumsances. He assured the press that the exchange had the legal power to act against any action that might endanger the integrity and accuracy of market dealings. He also announced that Souq Al-Manakh was to close by late October or during the first week of November. The financial position of the Gulf companies was under investigation as a first step towards a decision on whether to allow their shares inside the new stock exchange. Those of Kuwaiti companies were accepted for dealing. The Committee had, however, approved the circulation of the shares of eight Gulf companies, with the rest to be admitted later subject to the the provision of valid supporting details.

The eight admitted companies were: Arab Company for General Investments (Shua'a), Coast Company for Development and Investment, Bahrain International Bank, Bahrain and Middle East Bank, Iron and Steel Corporation, First Gulf Bank, United Gulf Bank, and Petroleum Products Company.[133]

The Stock Exchange Administration Committee applied the new circulation system called the Written Auction on many companies in July 1984. The new system adopted with some modifications the rules applied by a number of world stock exchanges, amongst others those of Manila, Hong Kong, Singapore and Sydney. Dealing in shares, under this system, was through the recording of supply and demand rates on display boards in the Hall. The auction bidding was by middle men or brokers, and the purchaser specified the number of shares he wanted to buy. The new system suited the nature of the Kuwaiti market and became a more effective alternative for the present and the immediate future than its predecessor. The main characteristics of the new system were:[134]

Prices opened at a specific ratio to the former price.

Changes in the share price were at fixed ratios, up or down.

The broker was banned from dealing with himself if there was another broker recorded at the same price.

The broker could not deal on his own account through his own office.

No transactions could be conducted outside the Hall. All transactions had to be recorded on the market display board, together with offers to buy or sell.

Strict equality was observed between dealers and brokers regardless of status or volume of trading.

The number of transactions contracted by the client was subject to a fixed ceiling; beyond that, the broker had to stand down to the next client.

The broker was fully responsible for completion of a transaction, transfer and payment.

If two brokers quoted the same price, one whose name was on the display board would deliver the goods.

At 10.00 a.m. on 29th September, an electric bell on the fourth floor of the new tower building accommodating the Kuwaiti Stock Exchange sounded to signal the move from the old to the new stock exchange. A crowd of dealers called on the market to meet the dealings manager in the presence of the market director and his deputy, and the circulation manager. At the start of business, only the representatives of accredited firms of brokers recorded with the stock exchange were allowed in while the crowd of dealers outside followed the transactions either outside the Hall or on closed circuit television. During the morning sessions on the first day of business under the new system, eleven transactions were contracted, a promising start. Information about companies was on display so that people wanting to deal in their shares could check the facts without relying on rumour and hearsay.[135]

The Kuwait Stock Exchange recorded a steady growth in deals each day. The volume of circulation for the third week of October 1984 rose to 1,769,593 shares, an increase of 649,490 over the previous week's 1,120,103, up 57.98 per cent. The value of dealings was KD 12,353, or 1.07 per cent lower than the week before, when the total value of shares reached KD 1,137,420, the outcome of 114 transactions in the shares of 17 companies. Business was spread widely over all sectors with the exception of the insurance sector, which did not move during the last three weeks of October 1984. Busiest was the banking sector at 65.5 per cent, followed by Gulf companies, property, investment, industrials, services and foods.[136]

The new stock market had no big dealers. Many had been declared bankrupt; others had found it difficult to settle their debts. The princes of the old market had been crushed by the crisis. Some found the new market too restrictive and rigidly disciplined, too much of a contrast to old trade customs, and they kept away. The old market had always been under their exclusive control; only they had been able to raise or lower prices. A single visit to the old market by one of their members was enough to send prices soaring tenfold. Hangers on who followed the moves of the great and watched their expression had earned incredible gains, simply by recording attentively the gestures and moods of those who controlled the market's movements.[137] The new system neutralised the role of the old bosses who had objected to the written auction procedure and the unit system in terms of volume of dealings.

The old dealers had wanted to continue acting as a mobile stock exchange, fully in command of the volume and quality of transactions whether at the market, at a private meeting, on an aeroplane or during their frequent visits to Europe and throughout the world.

The stock exchange director general announced that if those dealers wanted to do business at the new stock exchange, they would have to comply with and be bound by its rules. Respect for the rules was indispensable because, as he put it, 'Even casinos have rules.' He added that there was a lot of money in circulation in Kuwait, in spite of the debts created by the Al-Manakh crisis. All that had happened was that the money had changed hands. The crisis had affected only 7,000 people. The director general said he was looking for investors, not speculators. Failing to find the opportunity for quick gains, the big dealers stayed away.[138]

The new premises contained 68 brokers' offices. A number of mergers took place which left six broking firms out of the 17 which had worked on the old stock exchange.[139] Brokers' commissions were raised; registration fees for brokers also went up, along with the bank guarantees that the brokers' firms had to deposit. These fees were set at a minimum of KD 250,000 per firm and could go as high as KD 500,000 or even KD 1m.[140] At a meeting held on 14th October 1984, the Kuwait Stock Exchange Administration Committee fixed brokerage rates as follows. The rates below would provisionally apply as per categories of share prices set against them.

Categories of Share Prices	Brokerage Rates	
	Vendor	Buyer
Below 250 fils (KD 0.25)	¼ fils	¼ fils
From 250 fils to KD 1	½ fils	½ fils
From KD 1 to KD 5	2 fils	2 fils
From KD 5 and above	4 fils	4 fils

Brokers' firms took 80 per cent of commission due on all transactions concluded through their offices; the Stock Exchange received 20 per cent. Finally, all brokers were to charge the prescribed rates of commission, on the basis of which the Stock Exchange share was calculated.

Companies approved by the stock exchange were required to pay a registration fee of KD 10,000 plus 0.01 per cent per annum of the company's capital, as the new stock exchange had to finance itself. Trading was from 10.00 a.m. to 12 noon and from 5.00 p.m. to 7.00 p.m. Working days were from Saturday to Wednesday inclusive.[141]

The new stock exchange faced no mean challenge. The market was virtually dead, affected by the Gulf War, the reduction of oil output, cuts in public expenditure, and the crisis the market itself had suffered. In view of the hostility of major dealers, it was likely at first that share prices would continue their downward trend.

On 27th October 1984, the Kuwait Stock Exchange Administrative Committee opened its doors to closed companies, but ordered that for every four brokers' firms incorporated by the closed companies, one should remain.[142]

By mid-October the Disciplinary and Arbitration Committee was formed, consisting of the stock exchange director as chairman plus two members selected by the Administrative Committee. Presided over by a judge, the Arbitration Committee included also two members of the Administrative Committee. It was empowered to settle disputes arising from any transactions concluded at the stock exchange. Its decisions were final and binding.[143]

The last day of Souq Al-Manakh was 1st November 1984. Dealings ended at 11.30 a.m., when over 1,000 of the market's customers and owners gathered around a modest banquet which cost about KD 300, collected with some difficulty from the offices and the market fans. The last deal recorded was 500,000 shares of a Dubai company at 39 fils per share. Depression and gloom were evident. One guest said, 'When I came to this Souq for the first time all my possessions were a *dishdāsha*' (an Arab outer garment), beads and an Arab headdress. Today, I own KD 15m. This is a sad and deeply touching occasion as we remember with nostalgia and tenderness those happy days.' It was a time for reminiscence.[144]

Although 1st November was the date on the death certificate of this Souq, it had, in fact, died two years before, once the crisis came into the open. Al-Manakh was bliss to some and disaster to others. It will never be forgotten.

On the closure of Al-Manakh, *Al-Watan* wrote, 'The story of the giant Souq Al-Manakh which asserted itself and caused a violent crisis that shook the whole country has had far-reaching repercussions affecting the roots of social and political life in Kuwait. It has been a cruel lesson on a scale without precedent in Kuwait or the region as a whole. The contradictions and inconsistencies evident in decisions taken on the life of Al-Manakh, and all the solutions that have been suggested, serve only to demonstrate beyond reasonable doubt the fragility of financial and economic policy. The Al-Manakh crisis is the outcome of such haphazard dealings.'[145]

On 9th November 1984, the director of the Kuwait stock exchange announced the final closure of Souq Al-Manakh. As from 3rd November, all stock transactions of Kuwaiti and non-Kuwaiti companies whose shares were accepted for circulation by the Stock Exchange Committee had been carried out in the parallel market at the Trading Hall on the fourth floor of the Stock Exchange tower building. The Stock Exchange Directorate threatened legal proceedings against brokers not registered with the Exchange who conducted business, including the closure of their offices, on the grounds that they had contravened the conditions of their licences.

Earlier, on 14th October, the Stock Exchange Committee had issued a resolution to allow the Gulf companies which had not been admitted to the official market to have their shares circulated in a parallel market under the control and supervision of the Kuwaiti stock exchange, with the promise that any company that applied for admission and complied with the conditions would be accepted in the official Stock Exchange. An hour and a half was set aside every evening for dealings in company shares on the parallel market, from 6.00 p.m. to 7.30 p.m., *i.e.* after the end of the day's work on the official Stock Exchange.[146] By 30th November 1984, the number of Gulf companies admitted to the parallel market was up to 16. Official acceptance of the Gulf and closed companies on the official market was subject to the strength of the companies' balance sheets for 1984. The middle men who had worked in Al-Manakh were also admitted to the stock exchange, to be given training until they were qualified to work on the market. As from 3rd November, no transfers of Gulf shares were allowed except by way of an official coupon from the stock exchange. Eight companies were accepted on the official market and 29 companies on the parallel market as at 31st December 1984.[147]

The inauguration of the stock exchange on 29th September under the new regulations and the closing down of the Souq Al-Manakh on 3rd November were intended by the government to herald a stock exchange based on sound foundations and free from speculation, auctioneering and individual systems. This was a praiseworthy action on the part of the government. But was the government able to protect the new market from the former's defects and shortcomings? The general answer is in the negative. The old market suffered from the inflated number of companies, many of which were no more than fictitious names on paper, including Gulf, closed and even some Kuwaiti companies. Now there was a new stock exchange accepting all Kuwaiti and closed companies and gradually admitting the Gulf companies subject to easy conditions. The problem was not only granting such companies formal recognition, but their very *raison d'être*. The explanation given was that part of the assets of the dealers on Al-Manakh were in Gulf shares and that such assets had to have their value protected in the private settlements, *i.e.* in terms of bank guarantees. Indeed, even the stock exchange's director admitted, 'Had it not been for these considerations, I would have wished most of the Gulf companies a heartfelt goodbye. Even the eight companies that were granted formal registration earlier after the inauguration of the Stock Exchange were not fully sound and clean, but they were better than the majority. They realised higher profits and provided better management than others.'[148] The Kuwaiti companies registered with the stock exchange were weighed down under the same burdens as the Gulf companies. True, the new stock exchange banned speculation, manipulation, auctioneering and forward deals, but it carried the companies' ills and granted them formal recognition and this has produced negative results. The majority of these companies are utterly incapable of achieving their aims. Moreover, the new stock exchange has been born in difficult circumstances internally and externally.

Three months have elapsed since the inauguration and still the share prices are continuing downwards. There is no hope whatsoever unless the government intervenes to sustain prices. There is a possibility that the stock exchange may turn out to be a good investment in the future, one which may help the national economy and contribute to the development of resources both on individual and corporate levels. But that remains a matter of conjecture until external factors are removed, especially the Gulf War, and there is growth in the national income. The dealers have to become familiar with the new system, and the parasitic paper companies will also have to be weeded out of the stock exchange. It is to be hoped that from then, the market will continue its efforts to stay regular, to open its doors to all Gulf and Arab citizens, and to expand beyond its regional frontiers.

Notes

1. 'Souq Al Manakh Crisis, a new experience of an old phenomenon', *Al-Iktissad Wal-Aamal*, [Beirut: monthly magazine], October 1982.
2. R.G. Winfield, *Success in Investment*, (London: Murray, 1981).

3. Verbal information from a business man well known in Kuwait who was involved in this transaction, October 1984.

4. Written information obtained from the Economic Department in Al-Rai-al Aam [Kuwait: newspaper], December 1984.

5. 'The Collapse of the Kuwait Stock Exchange of a Turnover of US$ 90bn', *Washington Post*, 24.11.82.

6. *Atlantic Magazine*, May 1983.

7. 'Comparison between the Souq Al-Manakh Crisis and the New York Stock Exchange Crisis', *Al Seyassah*, No. 5439, 29.9.83, p. 9.

8. Research Department, 'Souq Al-Manakh . . . Where To?' *Al-Iktissad Wal-Aamal*, May 1982, pp. 24–5.

9. 'Story of an Illegimate Child who Surpassed the Legitimate Sons', *Al-Watan*, 3.11.84, p. 10.

10. See Chapter 3, p. 55–6.

11. Jāsim Al-Sa'dūm, *The Climate of the Crisis and the Crisis of Al-Manakh*, (Kuwait: Al-Rabīa'n publishing and distribution company, September 1984), pp. 76–7.

12. 'Chickens are Home to Roost for all Kuwaiti Dealers and the Country is Still Rolling', *Wall Street Journal*, 2.12.82.

13. *Al-Bayan*, 6.2.82, No. 630, p. 3.

14. *Al-Watan*, 3.11.84, p. 10.

15. 'Is the Crisis over on Kuwait's Souq Al-Manakh?', *Al-Majalla* [London political news magazine], September 1982, p. 44.

16. *Al-Watan*, 26.9.82.

17. Hazem El-Beblawi and Raid Fahmi, 'Role of the Stock Market in Kuwait Economy', paper submitted to the Conference on the Development of the Stock Market in Kuwait between 14th and 16th November (Kuwait: Kuwaiti Chamber of Commerce and Industry, 1981), p. 64.

18. *Atlantic Magazine*, May 1983.

19. Seminar on 'Forward buying in the Kuwait Stock Exchange' at the Conference on the Development of the Stock Market in Kuwait, (Kuwait: Kuwaiti Chamber of Commerce and Industry, 1981), pp. 274–300.

20. *Wall Street Journal*, 2.12.82.

21. *Al Iktissad Wal-Aamal*, May 1982, p. 25.

22. *Al Majalla*, September 1982, p. 44.

23. *Washington Post*, 24.11.82.

24. 'Collapse of the Al-Manakh Empire', *Al-Khaleej*, No. 1264, 24.9.82, p. 6.

25. *Al-Watan*, 3.11.84, p. 10.

26. *Al-Khaleej*, No. 1265, 25.9.82, p. 14.

27. 'Crisis Hits at the Heart of Social Structure', *Financial Times*, (Arab Banking Supplement, 2), 15.10.84.

28. *Al-Talī'a*, [Kuwait: weekly magazine], September 1982.

29. *Wall Street Journal*, 2.11.82; *Al-Talī'a*, September 1982.

30. Jāsim al-Sa'dūn, *The Crisis of Al-Manakh*, p. 87.

31. 'Mysteries of the World of Gulf Share Speculation in Kuwait', *Al-Bayan*, No. 628, 4.2.82, p. 3; 'Is the Crisis Over on Kuwait's Souq Al-Manakh?', *Al-Majalla*, September 1982, p. 44.

32. *Al-Khaleej*, No. 1264, 24.9.82.

33. *Al Mostakbal-Al Iktisadi*, [Paris: weekly magazine], No. 124, 11.9.82, p. 39; *Al-Khaleej*, No. 1267, 27.9.82.

34. *Al-Anba*, [Kuwait: newspaper], 18.8.82; *Al-Khaleej*, 18.8.82.

35. *Al-Watan, Al Qabas, Al-Khaleej*, 24.8.82.

36. Badr Sultān 'Īsā, 'Get the Market Out of its Present Crisis', *Al-Watan*, 9.9.82.

37. *Wall Street Journal*, 2.12.82.

38. *Washington Post*, 24.11.82.

39. *Financial Times*, (Arab Banking supplement, 2), 15.10.84.
40. Ismā'īl al-Shatī, editor of *Al-Mujtama'*, [Kuwait: magazine], September 1982.
41. 'The Government's Responsibility', *Al-Watan*, September 1982, p. 1 and 10.
42. 'What happened to the Al-Manakh Empire?', *Al Mostakbal Al Ikitssadi*, No. 298, 6.11.82, p. 15.
43. *Al-Khaleej*, No. 1265, 25.9.82, p. 14.
44. *Al-Khaleej*, 25.9.82; *Financial Times*, 15.10.84.
45. Sālih al-Sarī', 'Impact of Act 100/1983 on Position of Dealers in Postdated Cheques on the Share Market', Special Report, (Kuwait: Projects and Research Department, August 1983).
46. *Al-Watan*, 25.10.82; *Al-Khaleej*, 26.10.82.
47. Minister of Commerce and Industry in a statement at a press conference held on 21.8.82.
48. 'Trap into which Small Dealers in Gulf Shares Fell', *Al-Bayan*, 23.9.82; *Al-Khaleej*, No. 1267, 27.9.82.
49. *Al-Khaleej*, 2.9.82, p. 14.
50. *Al Mostakbal Al Iktisadi*, No. 124, 11.9.82, p. 39.
51. 'Kuwaiti Government asks its Joint Stock Companies to Purchase Kuwaiti Shares to Pump Liquidity into the Stock Market', *Al-Khaleej*, No. 1279, 11.10.82, 1 and 11.
52. *Al-Khaleej*, No. 1285, 17.10.82.
53. *Al-Watan*, 6.9.82.
54. 'Crisis of Souq Al-Manakh', *Al-Khaleej*, 29.10.82.
55. *Al Qabas*, [Kuwait: newspaper], 14.9.82.
56. 'Impressions on the Treatment of the Stock Market Crisis', Industrial Bank of Kuwait, KSC, 12.7.83.
57. *Al Qabas*, 14.9.82.
58. 'Decree of Act No. 57/1982, concerning forward dealings related to company shares', *Kuwait Al Yawm*, No. 1436, p. 2.
59. Resolution of the Council of Ministers, No. 46/1982, describing the Constitution of the Board for Arbitration in transactions related to forward dealings in company shares', *Kuwait Al Yawm*, No. 1439.
60. Resolution of the Council of Ministers, No. 49/1982, describing transactions related to forward dealings in company shares, *Modern Legislation — Acts 1982–83*, pp. 378–80.
61. 'Resolution of the Council of Ministers, No. 57/1982 with respect to the regulation of security bonds for forward share dealings', *Kuwait Al Yawm*, No. 1454.
62. *Kona*, [Kuwait: newsagency], 24.10.82.
63. *Al-Khaleej*, 17.10.82.
64. *Washington Post*, 24.11.82.
65. *Wall Street Journal*, 2.12.82.
66. 'What Happened to the Al-Manakh Empire?', *Al Mostakbal — Al Iktisadi*, No. 298, 6.11.82, p. 15.
67. *Al-Watan*, 20.10.82; *Al-Khaleej*, 20.10.82.
68. *Al Mostakbal — Al Iktisadi*, No.298, 6.11.82, p. 15.
69. 'Crisis of Souq Al-Manakh', *Al-Khaleej*, 10.10.82; *Al Qabas*, 10.10.82; *Al Mostakbal — Al Iktisadi*, No. 298, 6.11.82.
70. Ibid.
71. 'Crisis of Souq Al-Manakh in the National Assembly', *Al Khaleej*, 12.10.82.
72. *Al-Anba*, 10.10.82; *Al-Watan*, 10.10.82; *Al-Khaleej*, 10.10.82.
73. 'A Week to Solve the Crisis of Souq Al-Manakh', *Al-Khaleej*, No. 1281, 13.10.82; *Al-Anba'*, 13.10.82.
74. *Al-Khaleej*, No. 1281, 13.10.82.
75. *Kona*, 24.10.82.
76. 'The Crisis of Al-Manakh sequence . . . and the search for a comprehensive solution', *Al-Itihad,* 27.10.82, *Wakh*, [Bahrain: Gulf newsagency], 17.10.82; *Al-Khaleej*,

30.10.82.

77. 'Decree of Act No. 59/1982 concerning company share transactions concluded in forward dealings and the protection of the rights of debtors', *Kuwait Al Yawm*, No. 1446, p. 2.

78. Article 4 of Act No. 57/1982.

79. Article 2 of Act No. 59/1982.

80. 'The Kuwaiti Chamber of Commerce and Industry announces its proposals to solve Al-Manakh Crisis', *Kona*, 15.12.82; *Al-Watan*, 16.12.82; 'The Proposals of the Kuwaiti Chamber of Commerce and Industry are Good Start to End the Crisis', *Al-Itihad*, 31.1.83.

81. Ibid.

82. *Kona*, 15.12.82, *Al-Watan*, 16.12.82.

83. 'Alī Hasan al-Hamdān, *Kuwait and the Crisis of Al-Manakh*, (Kuwait: Umm Al Qura Bookshop, 1984), p. 110.

84. 'Decision No. 5/1983 issued by the Minister of Finance, with respect to the regulation of the functions of the Securities Fund for Forward Share Transactions', *Modern Legislation: Acts 1982–83*, pp. 394–6.

85. 'Crisis of the Shares', *Al Khaleej*, 11.4.83.

86. 'Impressions on the Treatment', Industrial Bank of Kuwait KSC, 18.7.83.

87. *Al-Khaleej*, 10.3.83, p. 1 and 13; *Al-Watan*, 10.3.83; *Al Qabas*, 10.3.83.

88. 'Act No. 75/1983 Concerning the Regulations on the Settlement of Transactions connected with Company Shares Forward Dealing', *Kuwait Al Yawm*, No. 1473; see too *Modern Legislation: Acts 1982–83*, pp. 355–65.

89. An explanatory note to the draft law for the regulation of the settlement of transactions related to forward dealings in company shares — *Modern Legislation: Acts 1982–83*, pp. 366–76.

90. The Assembly added the condition that approval was to be obtained from a quarter of the debtors, representing half the debts.

91. The Assembly substituted 'selling' for the word 'discount' mentioned in this Article.

92. 'Resolution No. 16/1983 with respect to the formation of the Board of Directors for the Organisation for the Settlement of Transactions related to Forward Dealings in Company Shares', *Modern Legislation: Acts 1982–83*, pp. 384–5; see, *Kuwait Al Yawm*, No. 1474.

93. 'Resolution No. 14/21, 1983 with respect to the Organisation for the Settlement of Transactions Related to Forward Dealing in Company Shares', *Modern Legislation: Acts 1982–83*, pp. 386–90; see *Kuwait Al Yawm*, No. 1478.

94. *Al-Khaleej*, No. 1463, 13.4.83.

95. 'Why previous laws failed to solve Al-Manakh Crisis', *Al-Anba*, No. 2789, p. 5.

96. Statement by the Kuwait Minister of Finance, 'Abd al-Latīf al Hamad, *Wakh*, 17.4.84, *Al Qabas*, 18.4.84.

97. Ibid.

98. 'Debate on the Issue of the Stock Market', *Al-Talī'a*, No. 844, 30.5.84.

99. 'Why the Three Previous Laws Failed to Solve Al-Manakh's Crisis', *Al-Anba*, No. 2789, p. 5.

100. Kathy Evans, 'Souq Al-Manakh Problem Edges towards Banking Doorstep', *Financial Times*, (Arab Banking supplement, 10), 15.10.84.

101. 'Optimism of Banking Community in Kuwait', *Al-Watan*, 2.10.82.

102. 'Tomorrow is the Final Meeting to Discuss the Proposals of the Kuwait Chamber of Commerce and Industry', *Al-Khaleej*, 26.6.83.

103. Sālih al-Sarī', 'Impact of Act 100/1983', August 1983.

104. *Al-Khaleej*, No. 1582, 1.8.83, pp. 1 and 11.

105. 'Act No. 100/1983, Concerning Provisions Connected with the Settlement of Transactions Related to Forward Dealings in Company Shares', *Kuwait Al Yawm*, No. 1492, pp. 9–10.

106. Explanatory Note to Act No. 100/1983, *Kuwait Al Yawm*, No. 1492, pp. 11–13.

107. 'Impressions on the Treatment', Industrial Bank of Kuwait KSC; 18.7.83; Sālih al-Sarī', 'Impact of Act 100/1983', August 1983.

108. 'New Complications in Al-Manakh Crisis, Three Gaps in the Law Causes Controversy', *Al-Khaleej*, No. 1603, 1.9.83.

109. 'Decisive Steps for the Implementation of the New Law in October', *Al Bayan*, 1.9.83.

110. 'Measures to Activate the Securities Market, Efforts not Subject to Mathematical Calculations', *Al Qabas*, No. 4302, 6.5.84, pp. 1 and 17.

111. Sālih al-Sarī', 'Impact of Act 100/1983', August 1983.

112. *Al-Watan*, 6.10.83; *Al-Khaleej*, 6.10.83.

113. Kathy Evans, *Financial Times*, (Arab Banking supplement, 11), 15.10.84.

114. 'The Biggest Offset Plan in the History of the Security Market's Crisis', *Al Qabas*, No. 4184. 7.1.84.

115. *Al-Khaleej*, 13.10.83; *Al Qabas*, 13.10.83.

116. Ibid.

117. 'Decree on the Organisation of Kuwait's Securities Market', 14.8.83, *Kuwait Al Yawm*, No. 1492, pp. 6–8.

118. 'Law to Organise the Securities Market', *Al-Watan*, No. 3064, 1.9.83, p. 7.

119. *Al Qabas*, No. 4184, 7.1.84.

120. *Al Qabas*, financial page, No. 4188, 11.1.84; *Al Qabas*, No. 4184, 7.1.84.

121. 'First Official Meeting in the Framework of the New Offset Settlement', *Al Qabas*, No. 4186, 9.1.84.

122. 'Repercussions and Reactions to the Comprehensive Offset Plan', *Al Qabas*, No. 4185, 8.1.84.

123. Centre of Information and Studies, 'Memorandum of the Kuwaiti Chamber of Commerce and Industry', *Al Qabas*, No. 4240, 4.3.84, p. 11.

124. See appendix 2 for an example of such advertisements.

125. 'A new move for the national economy to retain its status and effectiveness, and restore its activity', *Al-Rai Al-Aam*, No. 7345, 30.4.84, pp. 1 and 8.

126. *Al-Watan*, No. 3301, 1.5.84, p. 1, 'Decisions to Activate the Stock Market and Property Values', *Al-Rai Al-Aam*, No. 7346, 1.5.84, pp. 1 and 3; *Al Seyassah*, No. 5649, 1.5.84, pp. 1 and 17.

127. *Al Seyassah*, No. 5650, 2.5.84; *Al-Watan*, No. 3302, 2.5.84.

128. *Al-Anba*, No. 3122, 3.9.84.

129. His mother is the sister of the Emir of Kuwait and his brother is the Minister of Finance.

130. *Financial Times*, 15.10.84 (Arab Banking supplement, 11).

131. Ibid.

132. Kathy Evans, 'Monolithic Setting for Virtually Dead Market', *Financial Times*, (Arab Banking supplement, 12), 15.10.84.

133. 'Khālid al-Khurāfī in a press conference', *Al-Anba*, No. 3140, 23.9.84, financial page.

134. 'Kuwait Stock Exchange, from Chaos to Controlled dealing', *Al-Watan*, 29.9.84, p. 11.

135. 'Can the New Stock Exchange Bring Back Confidence to Dealers?', *Al-Anba*, No. 3147, 30.9.84, financial page.

136. 'Weekly Report of the Stock Exchange', *Al Seyassah*, 20.10.84, p. 5.

137. 'New Stock Exchange Puts an End to the Social Role of the Power Bosses', *Al Seyassah*, 22.9.84, pp. 1 and 21.

138. *Financial Times*, (Arab Banking supplement, 10), 15.10.84.

139. *Al Seyassah*, 22.9.84, p. 21.

140. *Financial Times*, (Arab Banking supplement, 10), 15.10.84.

141. *Al Seyassah*, 25.10.84.

142. *Al-Anba*, 28.10.84, p. 1.

143. 'Formation of the Disciplinary and Arbitration Committee for the Stock Market', *Al Seyassah*, 17.10.84, financial page.

144. *Al Seyassah*, 2.11.84, p. 7.

145. *Al-Watan*, 3.11.84, p. 10.

146. 'Opening of the Parallel Market, a Step Towards More Work Organising in the Stock Market', *Al Seyassah*, 5.11.84, p. 7.

147. 'The Securities Market', *al-Anba*, 17.11.84.

148. *Financial Times*, (Arab Banking supplement, 10), 15.10.84.

Bibliography

Notes on Sources

The main problem was insufficient reference material and few reliably accurate statistics. This was particularly true of the pre-1981 period when most share companies, particularly Gulf companies, were exempt from official control and lacked an organisational framework. Neither brokers nor stock offices on the Kuwaiti stock market kept sales records, ledgers, or entry books showing numbers of stocks sold, prices and price fluctuations. Similarly, in the UAE and Bahrain, government bodies paid no serious attention to market organisation and therefore official records for the stock market and share trading were virtually non-existent. It is only recently that records and documents have been kept.

I searched, instead, for original sources so as to extract reliable data from primary material. The original sources consulted for this work are: authentic documents such as corporate annual reports, articles of association and memoranda of association, Emiri Decrees, texts of laws and resolutions of an economic, commercial, financial, monetary and banking nature. Other studies were mostly too brief or related to only a particular aspect of this work; this applies to the studies submitted to the conference on the development of the stock market in Kuwait, which was held in 1981; although the studies contained useful papers, most of the material presented concerned Kuwaiti companies and the development of the stock exchange in Kuwait.

I have also drawn material from Gulf daily newspapers, the Kuwaiti press, and Arab and international newspapers. As newspapers sometimes resort to sensationalism with a disregard for accuracy, I have searched for accurate news reports and reliable statistics concerning the market and positions of share companies, as well as government statements.

One of the most important methods of collecting information was through personal contact and interviews. Meetings with officials and others directly or indirectly involved in the affairs of the market were particularly valuable.

Finally, shortcomings or contradictions in figures may be accounted for by lack of reliable and official sources.

Books

Bearle, A.A. and G.C. Means, *The Modern Corporation and Private Property*, (New York: Harcourt, Brace & World, Inc, 1982).

Bulloch, J., *The Gulf*, (London: Century Publishing Ltd, 1984).

Fenelon, R.G., *The United Arab Emirates, an Economic and Social Survey*, second ed. (London & New York: Longman Group Ltd, 1976).

Al-Hamdān, 'Alī Hasan, *Kuwait and the Crisis of Souq Al-Manakh*, (Kuwait: Umm al-Qurā Bookshop, 1984) [in Arabic].

Khouja, M.W. and P.D. Sadler, *The Economy of Kuwait, Development and Role in International Finance*, (London: Macmillan Press Ltd, 1979).

Al-Khujā, Muhammad and Sa'id Walid, *Stocks of Kuwait Companies, Analytic Study*, (Kuwait: Economic Association Press, 1974) [in Arabic].

El-Mallakh, Ragaei, *The Economic Development of the United Arab Emirates*, (London: Croom Helm, 1981).

Marjān, 'Izz al-dīn, *Encyclopedia of Kuwaiti Commercial Legislation*, (Egypt: Al-Ahram Commercial Press, 1979) [in Arabic].

Al-Rumayhi, Muhammad, *Oil and Social Change*, (Kuwait: Al-Wahda Publication and Distribution Corporation, 1975) [in Arabic].

Al-Sa'dūn, Jāsim, *Climate of the Crisis of Al-Manakh*, (Kuwait: Al-Rabi'an Publication and Distribution Co, September 1984) [in Arabic].

Al-Tuhaih, Salem Marzouq, *The Securities Market in Kuwait*, (Kuwait: The Amiri Diwan, Office of Research and Consultancy to his Highness the Amir, 1983).

Winfield, R.G., *Success in Investment*, (London: Murray, 1981).

Government Legislation and Decrees

Charter, issued by the Ruler of Dubai on 19.5.59, to incorporate the Dubai Electricity Company.

'Act No. 15/1960 — Commercial Companies Law', *Kuwait Al Yawm*, No. 276, 23.5.60.

Decree No. 19/1970 Incorporating the Sharjah Insurance Company by Charter of H.H. The Ruler of the State of Sharjah and its Dependencies Promulgated this 8th March 1970 under the Laws of State of Sharjah and its Dependencies.

'Act No. 32/1970 on Organising Trading in the Securities of Kuwaiti Public Companies', *Kuwait Al Yawm*, No. 806, 1970.

'Ministerial Resolution No. 10/1971 on Organising Trading in the Securities

of Kuwaiti Public Companies, *Kuwait Al Yawm*, 15.8.71.
Emiri Decree No. 78/1976 issued by the President of the United Arab Emirates, concerning the establishment of Emirates Telecommunications Ltd (EMIRTEL), *Official Gazette*, No. 41, 1976.
Sharjah Group Company, Memorandum of Association and Articles of Association, (MA and AA), Emiri Decree No. 133/1976 issued by the Ruler of Sharjah on 16.11.76.
United International Hotels Company, MA and AA, Emiri Decree No. 141/1976, issued by the Ruler of Sharjah on 21.11.76.
United Insurance Company, MA and AA, Emiri Decree No 24/1976, issued by the Ruler of Ras Al-Khaimah in 1976.
Gulf Investment and Real Estate Company, MA and AA, Emiri Decree No. 12/1977 issued by the Ruler of Ajman on 12.1.77.
Gulf Agriculture Development Company, MA and AA, Emiri Decree No. 105/1977 issued by the Ruler of Sharjah on 2.6.77.
Gulf Cement Company, MA and AA, Emiri Decree No. 24/1977, issued by the Ruler of Ras Al-Khaimah on 31.5.77.
Gulf Industries Company, MA and AA, Emiri Decree No. 133/1977 issued by the Ruler of Sharjah on 29.6.77.
Resolution No. 25/1977 dealing with the establishment licensing of Exempted Share Companies, exemption from the provisions of the 1975 Commercial Companies Law, (Bahrain: Ministry of Commerce and Agriculture, 1977).
Sharjah Cement and Industrial Development Company, MA and AA, Emiri Decree No. 31/1979, issued by the Ruler of Sharjah on 12.5.79.
Gulf Medical Projects Company, MA and AA, Emiri Decree No. 48/1979, issued by the Ruler of Sharjah on 8.9.79.
Gulf Financial Centre Company, MA and AA, Emiri Decree No. 57/1979, issued by the ruler of Sharjah on 8.9.79.
Sharjah Insurance and Reinsurance Company, MA and AA, Emiri Decree No. 68/1979, issued by the Ruler of Sharjah on 14.11.79.
Gulf Real Estate Company, MA and AA, Emiri Decree No. 12/1979, issued by the Ruler of Ajman on 30.12.79.
Mining and Industry Company, MA and AA, Emiri Decree No. 13/1979, issued by the Ruler of Ajman on 31.12.79.
Dealers and Stock Brokers Ordinance Law No. 1/1981, issued by the Ruler of Sharjah on 1.5.81.
Statement from the Dubai Government concerning the compensation of the shareholders, and the transfer to the Government of Dubai of the title to these shares, and that payment of compensation to shareholders began as from 1.1.80.
'Decree of Act No. 57/1982, concerning forward dealings related to company shares', promulgated 20.9.82, *Kuwait Al Yawm*, No. 1436.
'Resolution of the Council of Ministers No. 46/1982 concerning the Constitution of the Board for Arbitration in transactions related to forward dealings in company shares', issued on 6.10.82, *Kuwait Al Yawm*, No. 1439.
'Resolution of the Council of Ministers No. 49/1982, describing the transactions related to forward dealings in company shares', *Modern Legislation — Acts 1982–83*.
'Decree of Act No. 59/1982 concerning the transactions related to company share

transactions concluded in forward dealings and the protection of the rights of debtors related thereto', promulgated on 22.11.82, *Kuwait Al-Yawm*, No. 1446.

'Resolution of the Council of Ministers No. 57/1982, concerning the regulation of security bonds for forward share dealings', issued on 15.1.83, *Kuwait Al Yawm*, No. 1454.

'Decision No. 5/1983 issued by the Minister of Finance with respect to the regulation of the Securities Fund for forward share transactions', issued on 16.2.83, *Modern Legislation — Acts 1982–83*.

'Decree of Act No. 75/1983 concerning the regulation on the settlement of transactions connected with company shares for forward dealings', promulgated on 20.4.83, *Kuwait Al Yawm*, No. 1473.

'Explanatory note to the draft law for the regulation of the settlement of transactions related to forward dealings in company shares', *Modern Legislation — Acts 1982–83*.

'Resolution No. 16/1983 with respect to the formation of the board of directors for the organisation for the settlement of the transactions related to forward dealings in company shares', issued on 17.4.83, *Modern Legislation — Acts 1982–83* and *Kuwait Al Yawm*, No. 1474.

'Resolution No. 14/21, 1983, concerning the organisation for the settlement of transactions related to forward dealings in company shares', issued on 23.5.83, *Kuwait Al Yawm*, No. 1478.

'Act No. 100/1983, concerning some provisions connected with settlement of transactions related to forward dealings in company shares', promulgated on 14.8.83, *Kuwait Al Yawm*, No. 1492.

'Explanatory note to Act No. 100/1983, concerning provisions connected with settlement of transactions related to forward dealings in company shares', *Kuwait Al Yawm*, No. 1492.

'Decree on the organisation of the Kuwait Securities Market', promulgated on 14.8.83, *Kuwait Al Yawm*, No. 1492.

Federal Law No. 8/1984, Trading Companies in the United Arab Emirates, issued by the President of the UAE in the Presidential Court, Abu Dhabi on 20.3.84, and published in the *Official Gazette*, No. 137, April 1984.

Annual Reports

Annual Report and Financial Statement: Arabian Investment Banking Corporation Company, Bahrain, 1983.

Annual Reports: Ajman Cement, Ajman, 1983–84.

Annual Reports: Coast Investment and Development Company, Ras Al-Khaimah, 1982–83.

Annual Reports: Dubai Commercial Bank, 1965–70.

Annual Reports: First Gulf Bank, Ajman: 1983–84.

Annual Reports: Fujairah Cement, Fujairah, 1983–84.

Annual Reports: Gulf Agriculture Development Company, Sharjah, 1977–82.

Annual Report: Gulf Drug Industries Company, Ras Al-Khaimah, 1981.

Annual Reports: Gulf Financial Centre, Sharjah, 1980–83.

Annual Reports: Investment Bank, 1980–83.
Annual Reports: Gulf Investment and Real Estate Company, Ajman, 1977–83.
Annual Reports: Gulf Medical Projects Company, Sharjah, 1979–83.
Annual Reports: Ras Al-Khaimah White Cement and Construction Materials Industry Company, Ras Al-Khaimah, 1983–84.
Annual Reports: Ras Al-Khaimah Poultry and Fodders, Ras Al-Khaimah, 1983–84.
Annual Reports: Sharjah Cement and Industrial Development Company, Sharjah, 1979–84.
Annual Reports: Sharjah Group Company, Sharjah, 1978–84.
Annual Reports: Sharjah Insurance and Reinsurance Company, Sharjah, 1979–83.
Annual Reports: Umm Al-Qaiwain Cement Company, Umm Al-Qaiwain, 1983–84.
Annual Reports: United International Hotels, Sharjah, 1981–83.
South Figueroa Investcorp Limited, Private Offering by Arabian Investment Banking Corporation (INVESTCORP) E.C. Private Placement Memorandum, June 1983.

Official Studies and Official Reports

El-Beblawi, Hazem and Raid Fahmi, 'Kuwait Stock Exchange, 1946–80', IBM Papers, series No. 6, June 1982.
El-Beblawi, Hazem, 'Economic Dictionary, supplement of the Economic Bulletin', (Kuwait: Ministry of Finance, 1977).
Qasim, Habīb Ahmad, Minister of Commerce and Agriculture in Bahrain, paper presented to the 'Seminar on Reality of the Stock Market in Bahrain, held on 1st May 1984', (Bahrain, Bahraini Chamber of Commerce and Industry, 1984).
Al-Sari', Salih, 'Impact of Act 100/1983 on the Position of Dealers of Postdated Cheques on the Market', Special Report, (Kuwait: Projects and Research Department, August 1983).
Venerso, M. Frank, 'Stock Market Development in the United Arab Emirates', Preliminary Draft of Report, 7th June 1982, submitted to the Official Stock Exchange Scheme.
Interim Report, 'United Arab Emirates, Securities Market, Alternative Market Mechanisms', 24th March 1983, submitted to the Official Stock Exchange Scheme.
Report by a Group of Experts on the 'Formation of a Kuwait Stock Exchange', Initial Report submitted to the Ministry of Commerce and Industry, June 1970.
Studies Presented by Specialists and Experts during the 'Conference on the Development of the Stock Market in Kuwait, between 14th and 16th November 1981', studies published by the Kuwaiti Chamber of Commerce and Industry, 1981.
Central Bank of Kuwait, 'Ten-year Study of Kuwait's Economy', *Economic Survey*, 1969–79.
6th Annual Report, Central Bank of Kuwait.
Study by the Department of Economic Studies and Research, 'Offshore Banking

Units and Exempted Companies in Bahrain, 1975–82', (Bahrain: Bahraini Chamber of Commerce and Industry, 1982).
Paper presented by the Public Relations Committee to the 'Seminar on Reality of the Stock Market in Bahrain, held on 1st May 1984', (Bahrain: Bahraini Chamber of Commerce and Industry, 1984).
Report by the Department of Economic and Company Affairs on Exempted Companies in Bahrain, (Bahraini Ministry of Commerce and Agriculture, 21.6.81).
Department of Commerce and Company Affairs Publication (Bahrain: Ministry of Commerce and Agriculture, 1979).
'Public Companies in the United Arab Emirates', (UAE: Data published by the UAE Federation of Commerce and Industry 1982).
'Impressions on the Treatment of the Stock Market Crisis', Industrial Bank of Kuwait, KSC, 18.7.83.
Annual Report, Kuwait, Ministry of Commerce and Industry, 1976.
Annual Report, Bahrain, Monetary Institution, 1979–82.
Securities Group, Kuwait Stock Exchange, 1982, Fact Book.
'Kuwaiti Stock Exchange 1976–82', International Kuwaiti Investment Company.

Newspapers and Periodicals

ATLANTIC MONTHLY [US magazine]
May 1983.

AL-ANBA, [Kuwait: newspaper]
Price Bulletin, January 1983–January 1984, 18.8.82, 10.10.82, 13.10.82.
'Why previous laws failed to solve Al-Manakh Crisis', No. 3122, 3.9.84.
'Khālid al-Khurāfī press conference', No. 3140, 23.9.84.
'Can the New Stock Exchange bring back confidence to dealers?', No. 3147, 30.9.84, 28.10.84.
'The Securities Market', 17.11.84.

AL BAYAN [Dubai: newspaper]
Ghassān al-Sharīf, 'Mysteries of the World of Gulf Shares Speculation in Kuwait', No. 628, 4.2.82.
Ghassān al-Sharīf, 'Mysteries of the World of Gulf Shares Speculation in Kuwait', No. 630, 6.2.82.
Ghassān al-Sharīf, 'Trade into which small dealers in Gulf shares fell', 23.9.82.
Ghassān al-Sharīf, 'Decisive steps for the implementation of the new law in October', 1.9.83.

COMMERCIAL REVIEW MAGAZINE [Bahrain, Bahraini Chamber of Commerce and Industry]
No. 183 June/July 1981.

FINANCIAL TIMES [London: newspaper]
Kathy Evans, Arab Banking supplement, 15.10.84.
'Arab Bank Buys in Los Angeles', 3.2.84.

AL-IKTISSAD WAL-AAMAL [Beirut, monthly magazine]
'The Stocks Game in Kuwait', No. 33, December 1981.
Yusūf Shibl, 'Souq Al-Manakh crisis, a new experience of an old phenomenon', October 1982.
Research Department, 'Souq Al-Manakh . . . where to?', May 1982.

AL-ITIHAD [UAE: newspaper]
Muhammad Harasha, 'Crisis of Al-Manakh, sequence and search for a comprehensive solution', 27.10.82.
Ibrāhīm Ahmad, 'Proposals of the Kuwaiti Chamber of Commerce and Industry are a good start to end the crisis', 31.1.83.

JOURNAL OF THE GULF AND ARABIAN PENINSULA STUDIES, published by Kuwait University, 'Awad al-Hamud and Rifā'ī M. Rifā'ī, 'Role of the Board in Kuwait share companies between theory and practice', Vol IX, No. 35, July 1983.

AL-KHALEEJ, [Sharjah: newspaper]
Khawla Matar, 'Stocks in Bahrain "five" ', 11.3.82.
Nadīm Jawad, special supplement on 'Gulf Investment', No. 1194, 15.7.82, 18.8.82, 24.8.82, 20.9.82.
Khālid al-Bassām, 'Collapse of Al-Manakh Empire', No. 1261; No. 1264, 24.9.82; No. 1265, 25.9.82; No. 1266, 26.9.82; No. 1267, 27.9.82.
'Crisis of Souq Al-Manakh', 10.10.82.
'Kuwaiti Government asks its joint stock companies to purchase Kuwaiti shares to pump liquidity into the stock market', No. 1279, 11.10.82.
'Crisis of Souq Al-Manakh in the National Assembly', 12.10.82.
'A week to solve the crisis of Souq Al-Manakh', No. 1281, 13.10.82, 17.10.82, 20.10.82, 26.10.82.
'Crisis of Souq Al-Manakh', 29.10.82, 30.10.82, 10.3.83.
'Crisis of the Shares', 11.4.83; 13.4.83.
'Tomorrow is the final meeting to discuss the proposals of the Kuwaiti Chamber of Commerce and Industry', 26.6.83; No. 1582.
'New complications in Al-Manakh crisis, three gaps in the law causes controversy', No. 1603, 1.9.83, 6.10.83, 13.10.83, 30.11.83, No. 1692.
Profit and loss statement of 30.12.83 of Sharjah Group Company, No. 1849, 5.5.84, 24.6.84; no. 2030 10.11.84, 18.11.84.

AL-KHALEEJ NEWS [Bahraini newspaper]
1.11.83.

KONA [Kuwait: newsagency]
24.10.82.
'Kuwaiti Chamber of Commerce and Industry announces proposals to solve Al-Manakh crisis', 15.12.82.

AL-MAJALLA [London, weekly magazine]
'Is the crisis over on Kuwait's Souq Al-Manakh?', September 1982, No. 182, 6–12.8.83.

THE MEED [London: Middle East Economic Digest in association with the National Bank of Abu Dhabi]
Middle East Financial Directory 1983

AL-MOSTAKBAL AL-IKTISADI [Paris: weekly magazine]
No. 124, 11.9.82.
'What happened to the Al-Manakh Empire?', No. 298, 6.11.82.

AL-MUJTAMA' [Kuwait: weekly magazine]
September 1982.

AL QABAS [Kuwait: newspaper]
18.5.76, 26.3.82, 24.8.82, 14.9.82, 10.10.82, 10.3.83, 13.10.83
Muhammad al-Shīt'ī, 'Biggest offset plan in the history of the security market crisis', No. 4184, 7.1.84.
'Repercussions and reactions to the comprehensive offset plan', No. 4185, 8.1.84.
Muhammad al-Shīt'ī, 'First official meeting in the framework of the new offset settlement', No. 4186, 9.1.84; No. 4188, 11.1.84.
Centre of Information and Studies, 'Memorandum of the Kuwaiti Chamber of Commerce and Industry', No. 4240, 4.3.84, 18.4.84.
'Measures to activate the securities market, efforts not subject to mathematical calculations', No. 4302, 6.5.84.

AL-RAI AL-AAM [Kuwait: newspaper]
'New move for the national economy to retain its status and effectiveness and restore its activity', No. 7345, 30.4.84.
'Decisions to activate the stock and property markets', No. 7346, 1.5.84.

AL SEYASSAH [Kuwait: newspaper]
Fāys Karkūtlī, Special supplement on Gulf public companies, No. 4927, 17.3.82.
Ibrāhīm Qabāni, 'Comparison between the Souq Al-Manakh crisis and the New York stock exchange crisis', No. 5439, 29.9.83; No. 5649, 1.5.84; No. 5650, 2.5.84.
'New stock exchange puts an end to the social role of the power bosses', 22.9.84.
'Formation of the Disciplinary and Arbitration Committee for the stock market', 17.10.84.
'Weekly Report of the Stock Exchange', 20.10.84, 25.10.84, 2.11.84.
Khālid Ahmad, 'Opening of the parallel market, a step towards more organisation in the stock market', 5.11.84.

AL-TALĪ'A [Kuwait: weekly magazine]
September 1982.
'Debate on the issue of the stock market', No. 844, 30.5.84.

AL-TIJARA MAGAZINE [Sharjah: Sharjah Chamber of Commerce and

Industry]
No. 1 and 2, January–February 1983.

WĀKH [Bahrain: Gulf newsagency]
'Statement by the Kuwait Minister of Finance 'Abd al-Latif al-Hamad', 17.4.84.

WALL STREET JOURNAL [New York: journal]
Peter Trowel, 'Chickens home to roost for all Kuwaiti dealers and the country still rolling', 2.12.82.

WASHINGTON POST [Washington: newspaper]
David Attaway, 'Collapse of the Kuwaiti Stock Exchange of a turnover of US$ 90bn', 24.11.82.

AL-WATAN [Kuwait: newspaper]
26.3.82, 6.9.82.
Badr Sultān 'Īsā, 'Get the market out of its present crisis', 9.9.82.
Ahmad 'Ali al-Du'ayj, 'The Government's Responsibility', September 1982. 26.9.82.
'Optimism of Banking Community in Kuwait', 2.10.82, 10.10.82, 20.10.82, 25.10.82, 16.12.82, 10.3.83.
Ahmad 'Alī al-Du'ayj, 'Law organising the securities market', No. 3064, 1.9.83, 6.10.83.
Share price bulletin January 1983–January 1984; No. 3301, 1.5.84; No. 3302, 2.5.84.
Būr Subhī, 'Kuwait stock exchange — from chaos to controlled dealing', 29.9.84.
Būr Subhī, 'Story of the illegitimate child who surpassed the legitimate sons', 3.11.84.

Postscript

One of the most salient developments in the post-Al-Manakh period has been a general slump in share trading throughout the Gulf. This was alluded to towards the end of the book; however, the slump deepened and spread throughout 1985 and into the first quarter of 1986. Moreover, the slump has been aggravated by the dwindling revenues of the Gulf states as a result of the continuing fall in international oil prices.

The damage to the Kuwaiti economy, arising in particular from diminishing oil revenues — in addition to the grave effects of the Gulf stock-exchange crash — has been so serious that towards the end of 1985 the government was obliged to call in a joint team from the World Bank and the International Monetary Fund (IMF) to study, together with local Kuwaiti experts, the deteriorating state of the economy and to suggest a plan for reconstruction. Starting their job in December, members of the combined team set for themselves twin guidelines: determination of priorities for non-oil sectors, and the working out of ways and means to direct government spending so as to achieve maximum economic prosperity. In the meantime, short-term acute issues remain largely unresolved.

So far the government of Kuwait has been pumping funds into local banks to enable them to grant sufficient loans to large debtors and to help bail out industrial firms hard hit by vast losses sustained as a result of speculating on the stock exchange. These funds are largely low interest time deposits.

By the end of 1985 the position of joint-stock companies in general was as follows: 37 non-financial investment companies listed in the official stock-market established in 1984 following the final closure of the Gulf stock-exchange; and 33 Gulf share-holding companies.

In November the Minister of Finance told the National Assembly

Parliament) officially that only six of the 'closed' and Gulf companies were actually making a profit and that five companies had sustained losses greater than their paid-up capital; as to the remaining companies, he said, their capital had been eroded because of accumulating losses. The Minister's statement included a proposal for the liquidation of 25 'closed' companies and another for the merger of five 'closed' companies and 15 Gulf companies respectively.

Though the government decided to buy over stocks of 33 companies it by the stock exchange crash, most of the proposals presented by the government for the settlement of the complex problems arising from the collapse of the stock-exchange have remained the object of heated and prolonged controversies among members of parliament. The government has been keen to buy stocks of companies at market value to enable them to repay their loans to banks. It also plans to buy assets of liquidated Gulf share-holding companies and stocks of merged companies. The stumbling block is that many influential parliamentarians oppose the employment of public funds in this manner and equally oppose the pumping of government funds into the banks. Problems of this nature are not encountered in the other two Gulf states, the United Arab Emirates and Bahrain. Though Gulf share-holding companies were established in the UAE, the Gulf stock-exchange operated in Kuwait; this is not to say of course that traders in both the UAE and Bahrain did not sustain losses. Moreover, as in Kuwait, many people from all classes in the UAE and Bahrain suffered from the effects of the slump in the local property market arising directly from the Gulf stock-exchange crash. Since 1982 property prices and rents have been steadily deteriorating, hitting in particular the middle classes who depend on rents as a primary source of private income. The process has been aggravated by the termination of the service contracts of thousands of expatriates due to austerity measures made inevitable by shrinking oil revenues and the liquidation of private sector companies.

The consequent recession has also resulted in fewer domestic investment opportunities, which has encouraged the outflow of private capital. Two other factors enhanced this movement:

— Aggravation of the lack of confidence as a result of the continuation and escalation of the Iraq-Iran war, especially after the Iranian occupation of Iraqi territory adjacent to the Kuwaiti border.

— Hikes in the value of the US dollar during 1985, a matter which has encouraged investment in the dollar.

Generally speaking, the Kuwaiti government has been, since the collapse of the Gulf stock-exchange in 1982, particularly keen to follow friendly' methods in resolving the issues arising from the crisis. In other words it has been doing its best to keep the issues away from the courts. As such, it has inevitably resorted to the use of public funds, a matter which has provoked fierce criticism from those who believe that the broad base of citizens — as the real owners of public funds — should not be made to pay for the wrong doing of those individuals who are responsible for the crisis.

The overall picture of the Kuwaiti economy — and to a lesser extent those of the other two Gulf states — is one of recession in the private sector and austerity in the state sector. If the deterioration of international oil prices and continuation of the Iraq-Iran war can be considered major factors causing this state of affairs, the after-effects arising from the collapse of the Gulf stock-exchange cannot be any less important.

Index

Notes:
1. The following abbreviations are used — Co. for Company; Corp. for Corporation.
2. Sub-entries are in alphabetical order except where chronological order is significant.

Abu Dhabi *see* United Arab Emirates
Abu Dhabi Hotels Co. 76
Abu Khamsin *see* Kuwait and Gulf Financial Centre Co.
advertisement concerning forward dealings 149
advice, lack of, and Stock Exchange crisis 96
agriculture/food companies 24, 79
companies capital and shares 28, 29, 35, 37, 45, 64
companies characteristics of 31, 32, 34
companies profit and loss 45, 47
Ajman *see* United Arab Emirates
Ajman Cement 29, 34, 43, 64, 88
Al-'Adasānī, Muhammad Yūsuf 100
Al-Ahmad, Shaikh Jabir 108, 110–11, 115
Al-Ain Cement 76
Al-Astā, Bāsil 107
Al-Ayyūb, Salāh Ahmad 103
Al-Du'ayj, Ahmad 'Alī 99
Al-Fahd, Salāh 117
Al-Hamad, 'Abd al-Latīf 94, 99, 108, 123–4
Al-Ibrāhīm, Muhammad 107
Al-Jabrī, Hamūd 107–8
Al-Jat Market 54–8
Al-Jazira Contracting Co 28, 31, 35, 68
Al-Johara Market 69, 71
Al-Kandarī, Ahmad 107
Al-Khurāfī, Khālid 133–4
Al-Manakh *see* Gulf Stock Exchange
Al-Marzūq, Khālid Jasīm 91–2, 108, 109
Al-Muhannā, Ahmad 109
Al-Muraykiz *see* Kuwait and Gulf Financial Centre Co.
Al-Mutawwa', Jāsim 88, 107
Al-Mutawwa', Najīb 88, 107
Al-Mutawwa', Zayd 107
Al-Muzayni, Yusuf 'Abd al-'Aziz 36 *see also* Gulf Financial Centre Co.
Al-Sabāh, Shaikh Khalīfa Al-Abdullah 124, 127, 132, 133
Al-Sabāh, Shaikh Sa'd Al-Abdullah 99, 100, 117
Al-Saqr, 'Abd al-'Aziz 62, 99
Al-Saqr, Jāsim 103
Al-Shatī, Ismā'il 99
Al-Tajammu' Al-Dinī 93
Al-Turkī, 'Abd al-'Aziz 109
Al-'Uwaysi, Sayyid 'Ali Abdallah 74
Arab Co. for General Investments (*Shua'a*) 28, 40, 64, 78, 134
Arab Co. for Iron and Steel 30, 45
Arab Development Co. 28
Arab International Co. 41
Arab International Insurance 30, 42, 64

Arab Investment Bank 41
Arab Sahil Bank 24, 30, 40, 42
Arabian Investment Banking Corp. 30, 42
auditing firms and Stock Exchange crisis 98–101

Bahbahānī, 'Abd al-Jalil 36–7
Bahrain
public companies: achievements of 39, 40, 42, 43; characteristics of 33, 34; economic impact of 46, 48; emergence of 20–1, 23, 24, 28–32; *see also* companies, types of
Stock Exchange: crisis and 95, 110; emergence and development 67–73; Kuwait and 66, 70–2
Bahrain International Bank 30, 42, 134
Bahrain International Investment Centre 28
Bahrain & Kuwait Investment Group 28, 35, 41, 64
Bahrain & Middle East Bank 30, 35, 41, 42, 64, 134
Bank of Arab Coast 78
Bank of Oman 74
banks, Gulf 67, 78
achievements 39–43
capital and shares 30, 35, 64, 69, 72
crisis and 72–3, 127, 134
finance from 23–4
flourish initially 48, 68–70, 74–6
inflation and 49
profit and loss 47
see also financial companies
banks, Kuwait 5, 40, 78, 80
capital and shares 6, 17
crisis and 94, 99, 102, 119
finance from 14–15
Gulf companies and 30, 65, 74
reform of system 1
see also financial companies
borrowing 14–15, 23–4
by board members 36–7
Britain 49
British Bank for Middle East 1, 74
brokers
Gulf 60, 79
Kuwait 55

capital and shares *see under* agricultural/food companies; banks; financial companies; industrial companies
causes of Gulf Stock Exchange crisis 90–101
advice, lack of 96
auditing firms and falsified reports 98–101
coordination between countries, lack of 95
development plan, lack of 94–5
market growth without framework 90–3
new investors 95–6
oil output reduction 97–8
political and military developments 96–7
speculation and forward dealing 93–4
United States, high interest rates in 97
see also Gulf Stock Exchange crisis
Central Banks
Bahrain 70
Kuwait 5, 78, 80, 94, 99, 102, 119
UAE 42, 49
Coast Co. for Development and Investment 28, 35, 103, 134
Commission on public companies (Kuwait) 8
communications *see* transport etc
companies, types of *see* agriculture; banks; financial; industrial; medical; property; transport/communications
crisis *see under* Gulf Stock Exchange

daily press price lists 148
dealers 36
deferred payment system *see* forward dealing
development plan, lack of 94–5
dishonesty 93
Drugs Co. 41
drugs companies *see* medical
Dubai *see* United Arab Emirates
Dubai Commercial Bank Ltd 75
Dubai Electricity Co. 74

economic impact
of Gulf public companies 46–51
of Gulf Stock Exchange 63–6

on Gulf Stock Exchange crisis 90–6, 97–8
of Kuwait Stock Exchange 14–15
Egypt 40
Emirates Kalankar Co. 29, 34, 45, 79
Emirates Telecommunications Ltd (EMITEL) 76
'exempted' companies 68

false reports 98–101
fees, arbitrary imposition 38
financial companies
Gulf 22, 32, 41, 78; achievements 39–43; boards of 33, 36, 37; capital and shares 23, 25–6, 28, 30, 35, 64; crisis and 134; profit and loss 47; *see also* banks
Kuwait 3, 15, 41, 58; boards of 33, 36; capital and shares 6, 16, 17, 28; crisis and 102, 130; *see also* banks
First Gulf Bank 24, 30, 35, 40, 42, 47, 64, 78, 134
food companies *see* agriculture/food companies
Foreign Investment Corp. 13, 102
forward dealing/deferred payment 60–1, 79, 88, 93–4, 103
advertisement 149
legislation 104–28, 132
founders
majority shares owned by 37; private property attitude to companies 32–3
Frab Bank 69
France 40, 49
Fujairah *see* United Arab Emirates
Fujairah Cement 29, 34, 35, 43, 45, 64

General Corp. for Drugs and Medical Equipment 34
General Warehouse Co. 7, 14
government
intervention 101–33; lack of 90–6, 98–101
investment by 34
see also legislation
guidance, lack of, and Stock Exchange crisis 96
Gulf Agricultural Development Co. 24, 28, 32, 34, 35, 37, 38, 47
Gulf Animal Resources 24, 29, 34, 37, 45, 79
Gulf Cement Co. 26–7, 29, 31, 34, 43, 64
Gulf Drug Industries 29, 46
Gulf Financial Centre Co. (*Al-Muzayni*) 22, 28, 35, 36, 37, 41, 47, 64
Gulf Gas Exploitation Co. 24, 30, 34
Gulf Group for Projects and Industry 30
Gulf Industries Co. 26, 28
Gulf Investment and Real Estate Co. 25–6, 28, 29, 32, 35, 37, 40, 47, 64
Gulf Kalankar 29, 34, 64
Gulf Livestock 29, 34, 45
Gulf Medical Projects 29, 32, 35, 46, 47, 64
Gulf public companies (1976–82) 20–53
emergence and development 20–31
characteristics of 31–8
achievements of 38–46
economic impact and results 46–51
Gulf Real Estate 28, 35, 64
Gulf Riyal Bank 69
Gulf Stock Exchange 20, 54–85
emergence and development; Bahrain 67–73; Kuwait 54–63; United Arab Emirates 74–82
crisis 86–144; as first of its kind 86–7; start of 87–9; intervention 101–33; new Stock Exchange inaugurated 133–9; *see also* causes of crisis
Gulf Union Insurance 30, 42
Gulf United Bank 40

holding companies 49–50
Hong Kong 40, 134
Husayn, 'Abd al-'Aziz 62, 99

industrial companies
Gulf 22, 24, 31, 74, 76; achievements 43–6; capital and shares 26, 28–30, 35, 37, 64; crisis and 88, 134; founders 36–7; profit and loss 47; stated purpose ignored 34, 66
Kuwait 3, 4, 6, 14, 15, 17
Industrial Development Co. 44
Inflation

of share prices 49
risk diverted 14
information, lack of, and Stock Exchange crisis 96
insurance companies *see* financial companies
International Hotels Co. 29, 35, 41, 46, 64
International Insurance Co. 30, 43
international investments 49
International Nursery Farm Co. 45
intervention *see under* government
investment companies *see* financial companies
investment, Kuwaiti, in Gulf public companies 20–2, 55, 69, 71, 78–9, 95
Iraq-Iran war 49, 97
Iron and Steel Corp. 134
Israel 97

Jat Market 54–8
Johara Market 69, 71
Jumbo Bank 127

Kabazād, Abdullah Muhammed 107
Keynes, Lord J.M. 86–7
Khalīfa al-Abdullah *see* Al-Sabāh, Shaikh Khalīfa al-Abdullah
Kuwait
investment in Gulf public companies 20–2, 55, 69, 71, 78–9, 95
public companies (1950–80) 1–19; historical development 1–9; emergence 20–3; achievements 48, 50; characteristics 32–3, 36; *see also* companies, types of
Stock Exchange: emergence and development 54–63; organisation 9–14; effect on Bahrain 66, 70–2; effect on UAE 55, 66–7, 74, 78, 79–80; effect on economic and social life 14–15, 63–6; *see also* Gulf Stock Exchange crisis
Kuwait Bank 40
Kuwait and Gulf Financial Centre Co. (*Abu Khamsin/Al-Muraykiz*) 28, 33, 35, 36, 41
Kuwait International Investment Co. 6, 15, 16, 17, 58
Kuwaiti Corp. for Trading, Contracting and Foreign Investments 130
Kuwaiti Investment Corp. 17, 102
Kuwaiti National Bank 1, 6, 17, 74, 102
Kuwaiti Oil Tankers 2, 7
Kuwaiti Pharmaceutical Co. 14
Kuwaiti Real Estate Investment Group 99

Lebanon 49, 97
legislation (acts, laws, orders, resolutions) 151–3
1960 (No. 15) 2–3, 8, 9, 56, 90
1970 4, 5, 8
1975: (No. 28) 21, 68, 90; (No. 3) 8–9, 55–6
1976 9–11
1977 13, 68–9
1981 69
1982 105; (No. 57) 104–10, 111, 112, 119; (No. 59) 110–14, 121
1983 114, 116–17, 133; (No. 100) 120–8, 132; (No. 75) 115–20, 121, 122
1984 21
Emiri Decrees 22–7, 31, 33, 41, 49, 67, 76, 79
see also government
Libya 101
liquidity
decline 94
high 4, 14, 57, 70, 75
loans *see* borrowing
loss and profit figures 47

Manakh *see* Gulf Stock Exchange
Manila 134
medical and drug companies 29, 32, 34–5, 41, 46, 47, 64
military developments and Stock Exchange crisis 96–7
Mining & Industries Co. 24, 29, 34, 35, 37, 45
multiple board membership 37
multi-purpose companies 24–31

names *see* publicity
National Banks
of Abu Dhabi 75
of Bahrain 67, 72, 73

of Dubai 74
of Kuwait 119
of Sharjah 41
National Co. for Motor Cars Manufacture & Trading 6, 15
National Kuwaiti Cinema Co. 2

OECD countries 101
offset arrangements scheme 130–3
Offshore Kuwait International Co. for Petrol Investments 14
oil 1, 3, 4
boom 20, 56–7, 75, 77, 94
reduced output 97–8
Oman 23, 26, 32
Oriental Co. for Production and Distribution 29

parallel market, consequences of 65–6
Pearl Investment 28, 35, 40–1, 64
Petroleum Products Co. 29, 35, 45, 64, 134
political developments and Stock Exchange crisis 96–7
postdated cheques *see* forward dealing
Poultry and Fodder Co. 35
private property, founders regard companies as 32–3
professionals undermined by easy profits 66
profit and loss figures 47
profits, quick/speculation 93–4
in Gulf Stock Exchange 61, 63, 66, 70, 87
in Kuwait 23, 31–2, 34, 48–9, 57, 86–7, 90
property companies
Gulf 28, 31, 35, 61, 64, 68
Kuwait 5, 7, 99
publicity and names, obsession with 33, 34, 36

Qatar 23, 32

Ra'ad Foodstuffs Co. 45
Ras Al-Khaimah *see* United Arab Emirates
Ras Al-Khaimah Cement 29, 34
Ras Al-Khaimah Investment 28
Ras Al-Khaimah Poultry and Fodder 29, 35, 45, 64
Reagan administration 89, 97
Refrigeration Warehouses 15
religious groups 99–100

Saudi Arabia 32, 101
savings mobilised 65
Schultz, George 89
Sdīrāwī, 'Abdallah Jāsim 103
Securities Administration (Kuwait) 12
Securities Commission (Kuwait) 9–10, 11, 13
service companies *see* transport etc
shares and stocks
daily press price list 148
differential between face and market values 35, 38, 64
first trading in 2
prices (1976–82) 16–17
sales coupons, examples of 145–7
slump 63
see also capital and shares; Gulf Stock Exchange crisis; Stock Exchange
Sharjah *see* United Arab Emirates
Sharjah Cement and Industrial Development Co. 22, 29, 34, 35, 37, 43, 44, 76
Sharjah Group 22–3, 28, 32, 34, 35, 37, 39–40, 47, 64, 78
Sharjah Insurance Co. 41, 75
Sharjah Insurance and Re-insurance Co. 30, 42, 47
Singapore 134
social life, impact of Stock Exchange on 63–6
see also economic impact
Souq Al-Jat 54–8
Souq Al-Johara 69, 71
Souq Al-Manakh *see* Gulf Stock Exchange
speculation *see* profits, quick
Stock Exchange
Gulf *see* Gulf Stock Exchange
Kuwait: impact on economy 14–15; organisation of 9–14
new inaugurated 133–9
Sydney 134

Taqī, 'Abd al-'Aziz 109
transport/communications/services companies Gulf 28, 29, 35, 41, 45, 64, 76
Kuwait 2, 3, 7
Trowel, Peter 89

UAE *see* United Arab Emirates
Umm Al-Qaiwain *see* United Arab Emirates
Umm Al-Qaiwain Cement 29, 35, 36, 43, 64
undeveloped companies 33–4
Union Cement 76
United Arab Emirates
  legislation *see* legislation, Emiri
    public companies: achievements of 39–46; characteristics of 31–8; economic impact of 46–50; emergence of 20–8; *see also* companies, types of
  Stock Exchange: crisis and 71–2, 95, 103, 110; emergence and development 74–82; Kuwait and 55, 66, 74, 78, 79–80
United Gulf Bank 30, 42, 134
United Gulf Industry and Services Co. 28, 45, 64
United Insurance Co. 23, 30, 37, 42, 64
United International Hotels Co. 29, 35, 41, 46, 64
United States 40, 49, 86, 88–90, 127
  dollar values for shares 37
  interest rates 97
war, Iran-Iraq 49, 97
White Cement 43
World Securities Market 7–8